HOTSPOTS
LANZA

Written by Andrew Sanger
Front cover photography courtesy of Thomas Cook Tour Operations Ltd

Original design concept by Studio 183 Limited
Series design by the Bridgewater Book Company
Cover design/artwork by Lee Biggadike, Studio 183 Limited

Produced by the Bridgewater Book Company
The Old Candlemakers, West Street, Lewes, East Sussex BN7 2NZ, United Kingdom
www.bridgewaterbooks.co.uk
Project Editor: Emily Casey Bailey
Project Designer: Lisa McCormick

Published by Thomas Cook Publishing
A division of Thomas Cook Tour Operations Limited
PO Box 227, Units 15-16, Coningsby Road, Peterborough PE3 8SB, United Kingdom
email: books@thomascook.com
www.thomascookpublishing.com
+ 44 (0) 1733 416477

ISBN-13: 978-1-84157-525-4
ISBN-10: 1-84157-525-9

First edition © 2006 Thomas Cook Publishing
Text © 2006 Thomas Cook Publishing
Maps © 2006 Thomas Cook Publishing
Head of Thomas Cook Publishing: Chris Young
Project Editor: Diane Ashmore
Production/DTP Editor: Steven Collins

Printed and bound in Spain by Graficas Cems, Navarra, Spain

CONTENTS

SYMBOLS KEY

The following is a key to the symbols used throughout this book:

_i_	information office	✚	hospital	🍴	restaurant
🚌	bus stop	✈	airport	☕	café
✉	post office	↘	tip	🍸	bar
✝	church	🛍	shopping	🍷	fine dining

---

❶ telephone	❶ fax	❷ email	Ⓦ website address
❸ address	🕐 opening times	❶ important	
€ budget price	€€ mid-range price	€€€ most expensive	
★ specialist interest	★★ see if passing	★★★ top attraction	

INTRODUCTION
Getting to know Lanzarote

ATLANTIC OCEAN

LA PALMA

SANTA CRUZ DE
LA PALMA

PUERTO DE LA CRUZ

SANTA CR▸
DE TENERI

LA GOMERA

TENERIFE

SAN SEBASTIÁN
DE LA GOMERA

LOS CRISTIANOS

EL HIERRO

VALVERDE

NORTH AMERICA

EUROPE

CANARY ISLANDS

AFRICA

SOUTH AMERICA

LANZAROTE

ARRECIFE

PLAYA BLANCA

PUERTO DEL CARMEN

CORRALEJO

FUERTEVENTURA

PUERTO DEL ROSARIO

GRAN TARAJAL

JANDÍA PLAYA

LAS PALMAS DE GRAN CANARIA

GRAN CANARIA

UERTO DE MOGÁN

0	25	50 km
0		30 miles

Getting to know Lanzarote

If visitors to Lanzarote come looking only for sun, sea and sand, they will not be disappointed. This most easterly and most northerly of the Canaries is the sunniest and driest of the islands, and its beaches are among the best, with pale sand that in ages past was blown over from Saharan Africa, just 96.5 km (60 miles) away.

However, Lanzarote offers much more than that, thanks to a volcano called Timanfaya and a man called César Manrique. Both the man and the volcano have made this into a special land of huge contrasts. A quarter of Lanzarote's land area is a volcanic wasteland with its own harsh, fascinating beauty. The rest of the island is quiet and rural, but dotted with numerous curiosities formed by the volcanic past.

Around the sheltered southern shores, tourism has flourished. Yet due to the restraining influence of the artist Manrique, development has been carefully controlled. In 1993 the whole island of Lanzarote, including all its towns and villages, was declared a UN Biosphere Reserve in recognition of its unique character and the harmony of man and nature on the island.

THE RESORTS

There are three holiday resorts on Lanzarote, the island's capital making a fourth for a more authentic Spanish experience. The most established of the purpose-built resorts is Puerto del Carmen, south of Arrecife. The centre of Puerto del Carmen is a lively place, with many restaurants, late-night bars and discos. The resort extends into quieter, newer developments such as Playa de los Pocillos. On the other side of Arrecife is the second resort, Costa Teguise, which is arranged as a series of small *urbanizaciós* along the coast – some have a reputation as hideaways for well-off Spanish families, including celebrities. More remote is the third resort, Playa Blanca, steadily expanding on the southern tip of the island, which has some excellent beaches. All the resorts have good water sports facilities, with a choice of bars, restaurants and nightlife.

N

| 0 | 5 | 10 Km |
| 0 | | 5 miles |

MONTAÑA CLARA

LA GRACIOSA

ATLANTIC OCEAN

ORZOLA
MIRADOR DEL RIO
Corona
• Guinate
JAMEOS DEL AGUA
CUEVA DE LOS VERDES
HARÍA
ARRIETA

LA CALETA
FAMARA
670 m

LA SANTA

Jardin de Cactus

TINAJO
• Museo Agrícola el Patio
TEGUISE

MANCHA BLANCA
• Ermita de los Dolores
MOZAGA
TAHICHE

• Centro de Interpretación
COSTA TEGUISE

Parque Nacional de Timanfaya
La Geria
SAN BARTOLOMÉ
Fundación César Manrique

• Islote de Hilario
ARRECIFE

EL GOLFO
TIAS
PLAYA HONDA

YAIZA
UGA
MÁCHER
MATAGORDA

SALINAS DE JANUBIO
PUERTO CALERO
PUERTO DEL CARMEN
PLAYA DE LOS POCILLOS

FEMÉS
PLAYA QUEMADA

PLAYA BLANCA
unta echigera
Punta del Papagayo

ATLANTIC OCEAN

Timanfaya

The volcanic mountain Timanfaya, at 510 m (1673 ft), dominates western Lanzarote and is responsible for the bizarre landscapes of the 200 sq km (124 sq mile) Parque Nacional de Timanfaya. This is the Lanzarote *malpais*, the island's 'badlands' where human life is all but impossible.

Though snoozing at the moment, mighty Timanfaya is still very much alive. It last blew its top 250 years ago, blasting a large part of Lanzarote into an awesome landscape of blackened, twisted rock. Today the ground at the summit is still warm to the touch, with a temperature of over

🔻 *César Manrique's stylish former home*

600 degrees Celsius just below the surface. A trip to the top – whether by car, bus or on the back of a camel – makes for the unmissable Lanzarote experience. Look closely though, and you will see that the volcanic terrain is sprouting white and orange lichens, and tiny succulents with rose-tinted points poke out here and there from between the jagged rocks. Indeed, at La Geria on the margins of the *malpais*, enterprising farmers have discovered that grape bushes can survive here, their deep roots plunging to find nutrition below the level of the volcanic debris.

César Manrique

Few individuals have had as much influence on the culture of a place as César Manrique had on his native Lanzarote. Born in Arrecife on 24 April 1919, the young César lived in the capital until his family moved to the north coast when he was a teenager. His exceptional artistic talent was apparent from an early age. In 1945, Manrique left Lanzarote to take up an art scholarship in Madrid, going on to live in New York, returning in 1968 to his beloved Lanzarote.

Back at home again, Manrique became fascinated by landscape as a medium for art. The island's governing council gave him a free hand to use his creativity to turn the island's natural wonders into its best tourist attractions. His works include the Timanfaya developments, the Jameos del Agua, Mirador del Rio and many other sights.

César Manrique was also preoccupied with the potential of tourism for good or harm, and successfully argued for strict measures to protect Lanzarote's fragile environment and culture. His greatest legacy was a law that all new buildings on the island must be low rise and traditional in design. The walls must be white, the exterior woodwork green or plain varnished wood, or blue by the sea. The visual effect is astonishing.

César Manrique built his own remarkable home in volcanic rock 6 km (4 miles) inland from Arrecife. Outside is one of the most impressive of his colourful mobiles, which he had erected at key road junctions around the island. He was killed in a car accident near to the house in 1992, but his influence continues to ensure that Lanzarote is known as the Canary Island with style.

The best of Lanzarote

BEACHES

Gorgeous beaches of pure golden Sahara sand – not the grainy black
stuff more typical of the other Canaries – await you in Lanzarote. The
sun-baked beaches of **Puerto del Carmen** (page 57) make it the largest
and busiest resort, adjoined by its quieter sister beaches of **Playa de los
Pocillos** (page 47) and **Matagorda** (page 35). The most northerly of the
resorts, **Costa Teguise** (page 21) has five glorious sandy beaches and a
welcome cooling breeze. On the southern tip, **Playa Blanca** (page 39) has
perhaps the prettiest beaches, and sun-worshippers flock to the famous
Papagayo (parrot) beaches (page 43), probably the finest on the island.
The beach at **Caleta de Famara** hosts surfing competitions in November.

AWAY FROM THE COAST

The whole of Lanzarote has been designated a Biosphere Reserve by
UNESCO – aimed at maintaining its cultural heritage and protecting the
quality of life. Lanzarote has avoided over-development and the contribution that the late César Manrique played in turning the island's
natural assets into top attractions is unmatched. His works include:

- **Fundación César Manrique** His own incredible house built in the
  middle of a petrified stream of lava (page 83) .
- **Jameos del Agua** An exotic subterranean garden in an underground
  volcanic tunnel with an underground lake (page 85).
- **Jardín de Cactus** Extraordinary garden of over 1400 varieties of
  cactus in shapes such as wedding cakes and porcupines (page 78).

THE BEST OF THE REST

Cueva de los Verdes Enjoy a walk through part of one of the longest lava
cave systems in the world (page 87).

Parque Nacional de Timanfaya Stunning attraction created to protect an
area of volcanic activity which devastated the island in the 18th century
and also known as 'Fire Mountains' (page 79).

RESORTS
Places under the sun

ATLANTIC OCEAN

N

0   500 m

0   0.25 mile

Playa de
la Arena

**CASTILLO
DE SAN JOSÉ**

❷

CARRETERA DE LOS MÁRMOLES

AVENIDA DE NAOS

Bahía de Naos

PÉREZ GALDÓS

PÉREZ GALDÓS

TEGUISE

❺

El Charco
de San Ginés

**TOWN HALL
AND POLICE**

GENERALÍSIMO FRANCO

**TAXI
RANK**

**CAS
DE S
GAB**

LEÓN Y CASTILLO

**IGLESIA DE
SAN GINÉS**

DOCTOR GÓMEZ ULLA

✉

ℹ

VÍA MEDULAR

JOSÉ
BETANCORT

❹

ℹ

**TAXI
RANK**

GENERAL GARCÍA ESCÁMEZ

CORONEL
BENS

RED CROSS

CIRCUNVALACIÓN

❸

GRAN HOTE

BOLIVIA

ZARAGOZA

18 DE
JULIO

JOSÉ ANTONIO PRIMO DE RIVERA

AVENIDA FRED OLSEN

❻

TRIANA

Playa del
Reducto

GENERAL GARCÍA ESCÁMEZ

GARAJONAY

VÍA MEDULAR

SAN BARTOLOMÉ

❶
✈

Playa
del Cable

CIRCUNVALACIÓN

Arrecife
vibrant island capital

For a real taste of Spain, visit Arrecife (pronounced 'array-see-fay'), Lanzarote's waterfront capital. Home to half of the island's population, it makes few concessions to tourism and remains a bustling working town. It is the location of most of the island's commercial enterprises. The very genuine atmosphere and authentic feel of the town make a fascinating and enjoyable contrast with all Lanzarote's other resorts, and it is the only one where locals greatly outnumber visitors.

Arrecife was the birthplace and childhood home of the distinguished modern artist César Manrique. However, having been developed long before Manrique made his rulings about island architecture, it is the only town on Lanzarote with the conventional multi-storey modern buildings he deplored, including the landmark eight-storey hotel – Lanzarote's tallest building – standing on the waterfront.

Yet Arrecife also has many delightful, pretty corners and several important sights, including a surprising seawater lagoon at its heart. The town centre reaches right down to the seafront, where there is an excellent sandy beach, pleasant shaded waterfront gardens and an attractive promenade.

The capital has good hotels and makes an ideal base for exploring the island. The main street, Leon y Castillo, and its busy side turnings, offer some of the best shopping in Lanzarote. If you need to take a break, there are plenty of authentic tapas bars and restaurants.

Arrecife, which is the Spanish word for reef, dates from the early days of colonial settlement. It is guarded by two fine little waterfront fortresses, which still stand; one of them has now been transformed into a modern art museum. The town of Arrecife became Lanzarote's capital in 1852, having been gradually growing for some decades. Before that, it had long been no more than just a small fortified port serving the island's former capital, inland Teguise. To this day, many islanders refer to Arrecife as '*el puerto*'.

⏷ *Arrecife's waterfront*

THINGS TO SEE & DO
Castillo de San José (San José Castle) ★★★
Some 3 km (2 miles) out of town, this attractive little waterfront fortress is entered on a drawbridge. The date of its completion, 1779, is carved over the doorway. Two centuries later, César Manrique installed the International Museum of Contemporary Art. There is a roof terrace with great views, while downstairs there is an imaginative glass-walled restaurant and bar. ⓐ Carretera de Puerto Naos ☎ 928 81 23 21
🕒 Museum open 11.00–21.00; castle open 11.00–01.00

Castillo de San Gabriel (San Gabriel Castle) ★
Built in 1590 to protect Arrecife's harbour, the sturdy fortress of honey-coloured stone stands a few metres offshore on the reef that gave the town its name. Accessed via an attractive causeway, today it gives great charm to the busy waterfront. A small archaeological museum inside displays local historic items, including Guanche art. ⓐ Avenida Generalissimo Franco ☎ 928 81 19 50 🕒 Open Mon–Fri 08.00–14.00

Waterfront ★★★

East of the beach and west of the port, Arrecife's town centre reaches down to the sea in an attractive waterfront area with shaded gardens and a promenade. The pedestrian walkway extends as far as the causeway to Castillo de San Gabriel. Just a few paces inland is the oldest part of town and the main shopping district. ❸ Avenida Generalissimo Franco and Avenida Mancomunidad

El Charco ★★

The Charco is an inlet from the sea, forming a small, still lagoon of sea water in the town centre. Today encircled by a walkway and cottages, it was the original reason for building the town here. According to legend, Saint Ginés lived as a hermit beside the water and a fishing community grew up around his hermitage.

Iglesia de San Ginés (San Ginés Church) ★★

This dignified little 18th-century church of dark volcanic stone and bright white paint, attractively restored, honours the town's patron saint. Standing in a pleasant square beside the El Charco lagoon, it is still the centre of the old town, and the focal point for the locals' fiestas and celebrations. ❸ Plaza de San Ginés ⏰ Open for religious services only

BEACHES
Playa del Reducto ★★★

The town's excellent del Reducto main beach forms a sandy sweep along the shoreline close to the town centre. It has been awarded an EU Blue Flag for cleanliness and water quality. There are some facilities on the beach, including toilets, showers, phones and wheelchair access. Just across the road there are hotels and several bars and restaurants.

Playa del Cable ★

For the town's second sandy beach, follow the waterfront road past Del Reducto for 2 km (1 mile) to the residential district of El Cable, which fronts onto the sea and has its own 984 ft (300 m) long beach.

EXCURSIONS

Just 5 km (3 miles) from the Arrecife waterfront, leaving town on the Teguise road, is the unmissable **Fundación César Manrique**, the artist's museum and former home (see page 83).

SHOPPING

 Arrecife's main town centre shopping street is Calle Leon Y Castillo (known locally as Calle Real), which runs downs to the waterfront. Wide, busy and crowded with strollers, it is the very heart of town. Few familiar international chains can be seen, but instead the street is lined with smaller local shops. Many good shops can also be found in side turnings off the main street.

Duty-free discount stores
Many shops offer electrical and photographic goods at low, duty-free prices. Beware of fakes and goods not protected by guarantee. One of the most reliable is Visanta. ⓐ Avenida Rafael Gonzalez 1

Art & antiques
Subasta is an appealing antiques shop just off the main shopping street. The helpful owner is a mine of information. ⓐ Calle Otilia Díaz ⓣ 828 08 10 00

Shopping centres
El Mercadillo, in Calle Leon Y Castillo, is the town's simple and appealing four-storey shopping centre. Inside is a diverse array of supermarkets, fashions boutiques, perfumeries and jewellers, leatherware specialists, craft shops and stores selling electrical goods at discount prices. For locals, one of the island's main shopping venues is the large indoor mall of Deiland Shopping Centre in Playa Honda, west of town. As well as a wide range of shops, it contains cafés and a cinema.

RESTAURANTS (see map on page 14)

El Cable €€ ❶ With tables set out on a terrace close to the beach at El Cable, west of the town centre, this restaurant offers a range of good meat and fish dishes in Spanish style. ⓐ Ciudad Jardin, Playa del Cable ❶ 928 80 56 49 ⓛ Open noon–midnight

Castillo de San José €€€ ❷ This elegant and unusual restaurant occupies the lower floor of the modern art museum now housed inside the former fortress. Designed by Manrique with his usual flair, this imaginative glass-walled restaurant and bar offers a wide variety of excellent local and international dishes, well prepared, attractively presented and served in a remarkable setting. There is an all-black theme – including black napkins. Smart casual dress preferred. ⓐ Carretera de Puerto Naos ❶ 928 81 23 21 ⓛ Open 11.00–01.00

Chino de Taiwan € ❸ Prices are reasonable at this much-liked Chinese restaurant and takeaway. Good food and service. ⓐ Calle Canalejas 52 ❶ 928 80 53 47 ⓛ Open 12.30–16.00 and 19.30–midnight

Domus Pompeii €€ ❹ Authentic Italian cooking is served in this convivial restaurant, with an excellent choice of dishes extending beyond the usual pizza and pasta. ⓐ Calle Jose Betancort 19 ❶ 928 81 42 16 ⓦ www.domuspompei.com ⓛ Open 12.30–16.30 and 20.00–midnight

El Leito de Proa €€ ❺ This bar and restaurant beside the waters of El Charco is very popular with locals. ⓐ Ribera del Charco 2 ❶ 928 80 20 66 ⓛ Open noon–16.00 and 19.00–23.00

Restaurante Hotel Lancelot €€ ❻ The restaurant of this pleasant little hotel across the road from Playa El Reducto is a useful resource. It is open to the public and serves decent international fare at reasonable prices. ⓐ Avenida Mancomunidad 9 ❶ 928 80 50 90 ⓛ Open for lunch and dinner

NIGHTLIFE

Nightlife in Arrecife is unlike what you will find in the island's three other main resorts. Instead of discos and folklore shows, the capital offers authentic evening entertainment for mainly Spanish adult audiences.

Regular bars usually stay open until the early hours. Discos generally open at around 23.00 and close at about 05.00. Instead of music from chart-topping UK bands, you will hear Spanish and Latin American music with a salsa rhythm.

The main area for discos and nightlife is Calle Jose Antonio in the town centre. In addition, the many clubs in Puerto del Carmen are just a few minutes drive away. Popular Arrecife venues include:

Disco Pub La Panadería ⓐ Jose Antonio 69–71 ⓣ 609 41 72 13
La Cervecería ⓐ Avda Fred Olsen, Edificio el Islote 6 ⓣ 928 81 73 22
Rincón del Majo ⓐ El Charco de San Ginés

Costa Teguise
sun, sand and sport

With its airy sense of space, five beaches, a wide range of sports facilities and excellent accommodation, Costa Teguise (pronounced 'teg-easy') has plenty of appeal. With an eye to Manrique's principles, the development has been cleverly zoned into green, residential and tourist areas. Purpose built on formerly empty sands just 5 km (3 miles) along the coast from Arrecife, it is now Lanzarote's second-largest resort and a favourite for upmarket, self-catering holidays, as well as having some of the island's very best hotels. Many regular visitors – including wealthy Spanish families – have bought holiday homes here. It is also ideally placed for touring and sightseeing in the north of the island.

Arranged as a ribbon of small commercial centres and *urbanizacións* clinging to the seashore, Costa Teguise has different beach areas that feel quite separate from each other. The resort has aimed for a restrained and functional style: a single wide main road – Avenida del Mar in the southern half and Avenida de las Islas Canarias in the northern half – links the different districts, lined with plain and simple low-rise blocks beside the sea. It is a pity, though, that the sea cannot be seen from the road: you must use the extensive parking areas and walk between the commercial centres to reach the beaches.

Although lacking an authentic town centre or old quarter, Costa Teguise has managed to create a pleasant focus around the junction of Avenida del Jablillo and Avenida de las Islas Canarias close to little Playa del Jablillo and a few paces from the southern end of Playa de las Cucharas. This is the only place where a road reaches the sea, and there is a lively atmosphere at this point, with many shops, hotels and a variety of restaurants. Here, too, is the attractive and crowded little pedestrian square Plaza Pueblo Marinero, where visitors congregate in the balmy evening air.

◀ *Costa Teguise beaches are sandy and well protected*

THINGS TO SEE & DO

Parque Acua Lanza (Aqua Park) ★

Just follow the signs that lead away from the seafront to this enjoyable waterpark at the back of the town. With colourful water slides and flumes, gentle rides for the youngest toddlers, more thrilling options for teenagers and adults, a bouncy castle, a lovely pool and sunbathing area, it makes a great excursion for all the family. The water is not heated – and can be too cold for comfort in winter. There are cafés and a gift shop on the site. ⓐ Avda Club De Golf ⓣ 928 59 21 28 ⓛ Open 10.00–18.00

Golfing ★★★

This unusual and attractive 18-hole **Costa Teguise Golf Club** on the northern edge of town, designed by John Harris in 1978 and considered one of the great places in the world to play golf, is open to visitors at all levels. Lessons and equipment hire are available. This is still the only golf course on Lanzarote, its green turf making a striking sight among cacti, palms, big geraniums and the brilliant sea and sky. The charming and comfortable clubhouse has a civilized air. ⓐ Avenida del Golf ⓣ 928 59 05 12 ⓔ lanzarotegolf@lanzarote.com ⓦ www.lanzarote-golf.com

Trekking ★★

Lanzarote's network of footpaths gives unique insight into this curious environment. **Canary Trekking**, based at Costa Teguise, puts together guided walks not just for the immediate area but for all the different types of terrain around the island. ⓐ Calle La Laguna 18 – Casa 1 ⓣ 609 53 76 84 (mobile)

Surfing ★★

Surf's up in Costa Teguise, where surfboarding and sail-boarding – and variations such as kite-surfing and surfaris – are immensely popular. **Lanzarote F2 Surf**, at the southern end of the main beach, Playa de las Cucharas, rent all equipment by the hour or by the day and give tuition in a choice of languages for new surfers. ⓐ Centro Comercial, Puerto Tahiche ⓣ 928 59 19 74

Windsurfing ★★

Windsurf courses at all levels are available in several languages and offer the International Basic Windsurf Certificate, along with board rentals. **Windsurf Paradise** are based on the beach at Las Cucharas. If you book in advance you can specify the type of board you require. Trips to Famara are organized with an experienced instructor. ⓐ Calle La Corvina 8 ① 928 34 60 22

Diving ★★★

The long-established, amply qualified **Calipso Diving** is a top name in Lanzarote diving and scuba. The beginners' courses are based at Costa Teguise, while other locations are used for the more advanced divers. Most of the dives are from the shore, and explore a varied and interesting underwater landscape of volcanic scenery, coral, wrecks and abundant exotic marine life. Advance booking is essential. ⓐ Centro Comercial Nautical, Avenida de los Islas Canarias ① 928 59 08 79 ⓔ Calipso@arrakis.es ⓦ www.calipso-diving.com ⓛ Mon–Sat 09.00– 18.00, closed Sun

Cycling ★★

The rolling landscape of Lanzarote make cycling an ideal way to see the island.
Hot Bike You can rent bikes for any period from half a day to a week or two weeks here. This centrally located shop can also provide maps, babyseats and other useful items. They also organize group excursions and guided biking tours of the island. ⓐ Playa de las Cucharas ① 928 59 03 04.
Tommy's Bikes The best-known cycle firm in town. This is where you can hire top-quality touring, racing and mountain bikes. They are generous with their time and advice and provide helpful maps and other informa-tion. They also organize full-day island tours and excursions, complete with sections that make use of jeeps and boats where this is necessary. ⓐ Situated near Playa del Jablillo, Appartements Galeon Playa, Calle de la Galeta 16 ① 928 59 23 27 ⓦ www.tommys-bikes.com

BEACHES
Playa del Jablillo, Playa Bastián and Playa del Ancia ★★
All these beaches are south of the centre of Costa Teguise. They are small, breezy bays of sand and shingle backed by hotels and good-quality residential housing.

Playa de las Cucharas ★★
The main beach is a long, sandy stretch with gardens, restaurants and hotels behind. This is the main area for windsurfing and water sports.

Playa de los Charcos ★
At the northern end of the resort, Los Charcos is a smaller sandy bay protected by breakwaters.

SHOPPING

Craft market
Plaza Pueblo Marinero is the focal point of an enjoyable craft market every Friday evening. Many of the stallholders can also be seen at the Sunday morning market at Teguise, selling items such as jewellery, pottery, stone-carvings and colourful hand-crafted souvenirs.

Commercial centres
Because of its closeness to the larger centre of Arrecife, shopping in Costa Teguise may seem limited. Visitors here will find that most shops are inside indoor *centro comercial* (commercial centres) selling beachwear, sports equipment, low-cost electrical goods and souvenirs, as well as food including fresh produce. The largest is behind Playa de las Cucharas.

○ *Craft market at Teguise*

EXCURSIONS

All the sights of northern Lanzarote can be easily reached from Costa Teguise, and excursions are offered by most tour operators. Driving independently, the Tahiche road leads to the **Fundación César Manrique** (see page 83) in just 5 km (3 miles). From here it is another 6 km (4 miles) to visit the island's former capital **Teguise** (see page 77).

Leaving Costa Teguise on the Guatiza road, the **Jardín de Cactus** is on the right after 10 km (6 miles). In the same direction, about 5 km (3 miles) further, are **Arrieta** (see page 87), **Cueva de los Verdes** (see page 87) and **Jameos del Agua** (see page 85).

RESTAURANTS (see map opposite)

Restaurants in Costa Teguise cluster into three distinct areas – Playa de las Cucharas, in the north of the resort; Playa del Jablillo and Plaza Pueblo Marinero, in the town centre, with many inexpensive eateries; and Playa Bastían at the southern end of the resort. It is easy to find an inexpensive meal or snack at any time at the café-bars behind the beaches.

Casa Blanca €€ **❶** This unusual grill restaurant in the Avenida del Jablillo area is in a charming little detached building with the kitchen open to view. It is surrounded by an enclosed terrace with wooden tables where local fish and salads, as well as classic meat dishes, are served. **ⓐ** Calle las Olas 4 **ⓞ** 928 59 01 55 **ⓛ** Open 18.30–23.30

La Chimenea €€ **❷** Among the many restaurants and bars alongside Las Cucharas beach, this one stands out for its good Italian food. **ⓐ** Centro Comercial las Cucharas, Avenida de las Islas Canarias **ⓞ** 928 59 08 37 **ⓛ** Open for lunch and dinner

Costa Teguise Golf Club €€ **❸** An unusual and enjoyable choice for a snack or a meal is the quiet, charming clubhouse restaurant of Lanzarote's golf course, on the edge of town. **ⓐ** Avenida del Golf **ⓞ** 928 59 05 12 **ⓦ** www.lanzarote-golf.com **ⓛ** Open for lunch

La Graciosa €€€ ❹ This luxury restaurant is inside the smartest hotel on the island – the 5-star Gran Melía Salinas Garden Village. A wooden walkway leads through tropical gardens into an elegant setting with live music, where the finest French cuisine is served. There are also dishes inspired by traditional local cooking, such as fish *à la sal con dos mojos*. Exceptional desserts. ⓐ Gran Melia Salinas Garden Village, Avenida de las Islas Canarias ❶ 928 59 00 40 ⓔ comercial.gran.melia.salinas@solmelia.es ⓦ www.solmelia.com

La Jordana €€€ ❺ In the Playa Bastián part of the resort, this is one of Costa Teguise's best restaurants, with folksy country-style decor and a fish-oriented menu that gives a local flavour to high-quality international cooking. ⓐ Calle Los Geranios 1–11 ❶ 928 59 03 28 ❶ Open 10.00–23.00, closed Sun

Montmartre €€€ ❻ A slightly tongue-in-cheek copy of a Parisian restaurant on the edge of town, but the skilful cooking of fine dishes such as duck liver pâté, and chicken stuffed with prawns with white wine sauce, provides the genuine feel of France. ⓐ Avenida de las Palmeras, near corner of Calle Los Geranios ❶ 928 59 12 05 ❶ Open 19.00–23.00 and lunchtime at weekends

El Patio € ❼ In the crowded pedestrian plaza near Jablillo beach, this inexpensive restaurant with its tables under a green awning is exceptionally good value for money, with authentic Spanish and Canarian cooking at modest prices. ⓐ Plaza Pueblo Marinero ❶ Open for lunch and dinner

El Pescador € ❼ In a corner of the attractive little pedestrian plaza at the heart of Costa Teguise, this good seafood and fish restaurant offers a cool, quiet haven. Decor reflects the marine menus. Service is friendly and professional. Booking ahead is advisable, especially on Friday night (market night in the square). ⓐ Plaza Pueblo Marinero ❶ 928 59 08 74 ❶ Open 13.30–16.00 and 21.00–23.00

Portobello €€ **②** Excellent food and service are available at this popular restaurant at Las Cucharas beach. ⓐ Centro Comercial las Cucharas, Avenida de las Islas Canarias ❶ 928 59 02 41 ❸ Open Tues–Sun 13.00–midnight, closed Mon

La Provence €€ **❽** Despite a sign promising '*Cocina Francesca*', you will find Mexican, Italian and Spanish dishes here as well as a few from Provence. Top favourites are the huge T-bone steaks, good pizzas and tasty garlic bread. Delicious home-made sauces. ⓐ Avenida del Jablillo ❸ Open all day

San Remo € **❾** Among many similar inexpensive eateries in this area, this reliable Italian restaurant has excellent pizzas and other popular dishes. ⓐ Avenida del Jablillo ❶ 928 59 02 85

La Terraza €€ **②** The menu at this bar-restaurant with outdoor tables close to Playa de las Cucharas is geared to holiday tastes. There is an extensive children's menu with a choice of meals at low prices. ⓐ Centro Comercial las Cucharas, Avenida de las Islas Canarias 20 ❶ 928 59 14 00 ❸ Open all day

NIGHTLIFE

There are many bars and pubs, some with entertainment, around Playa Cucharas, Plaza Pueblo Marinero and Toca shopping centre (Centro Comercial Toca) on Avenida de las Islas Canarias. Many visitors to Costa Teguise feel that it is worth taking a taxi into Arrecife (5 km/3 miles), or even to Puerto del Carmen (16 km/10 miles), for evening entertainment.

Bar-restaurants **Cactus Jack's** and **Legends** are the most popular late-night entertainment venues, with stage acts such as drag shows and tribute bands. Both are in Calle Acacias and open daily from breakfast time until the small hours each night.

Other established evening venues are the **Robinson Beach Club** and the **Columbus Tavern**, both at the Las Cucharas commercial centre. Lively pubs around Plaza Pueblo Marinero include **Hooks** and the **Irish Fiddler**.

Famara
open spaces and unspoiled beaches

For a taste of the simple life, unspoiled and protected Famara on the north coast makes a striking contrast with the busy resorts of the southern and eastern coasts. One of Lanzarote's best beaches is here, the 9 km (5.5 mile) golden stretch of Playa de Famara. The spectacular Risco de Famara (Famara Cliffs), rising almost sheer behind the sands, create a dramatic backdrop soaring to 450 m (1476 ft). From the cliff top, glorious views gaze out to sea and to the offshore islands.

Visitors to Famara appreciate the wild, natural feel of the place, while many locals continue to work as farmers and fisherman. What has prevented further development here is the fact that Lanzarote's north coast has rather changeable weather and the steady breeze of the trade wind from the north-west. The ocean is more risky here, too, with some of the biggest waves anywhere around the island and strong eddies and undercurrents. However, experienced windsurfers, divers and anglers love the place. Hang-gliding is another popular activity, as enthusiasts launch themselves from the top of the Famara cliffs.

Famara is also known as Lanzarote's naturist resort. About half the length of **Playa de Famara** is open to naturists, who can experience total freedom and privacy in this natural setting. Sunbathers – with or without bathing suits – find shelter from sun and wind in small horseshoe-shaped enclosures of stone at the back of the beach (similar to the *zocos* used on the island to protect grape vines).

La Caleta de Famara is a small harbour village and an easy-going and uncommercialized resort at one end of Playa de Famara. It offers a wide choice of locally owned self-catering accommodation and an authentic village atmosphere. Close by, the attractive Famara *urbanización* is a self-catering holiday village of semi-circular bungalows, with its own restaurants and small shops.

◐ *Famara's dramatic beach*

THINGS TO SEE & DO
Surfing
Famara is considered one of Europe's best locations for surfing due to its wave consistency, sandy beach, reliable warm air and water temperatures all year round, as well as its attractive physical setting. With these advantages, Famara is considered suitable for surfing all year round. The small beach of Playa de San Juan, west of La Caleta, is also a favourite with surfers.

The resort is ideal for many similar sports, especially kitesurfing, in which surfers are pulled along at speed and lifted out of the water by brightly coloured kites harnessed to their bodies.

Calimasurf ★★★
If you want to surf, surf, surf throughout your stay on the island, Calima's surf schools and surf camps at La Caleta de Famara provide residential holiday courses, including 'surfaris' for different levels of ability. Stay for 1–3 weeks, with people at the same level as yourself. The instructors are also qualified lifeguards. ⓐ Calle Achique 14 ❶ 626 91 33 69 ⓔ info@calimasurf.com Ⓦ www.calimasurf.com ❺ Open 10.00–21.00

Surf School Lanzarote ★★★
This top surfing school has over 20 years of experience on the island, and carries the British Surfing Association's highest award (it is the only BSA Level 4 approved surf school outside the UK). Its highly qualified instructors (all of whom are also qualified lifeguards) use the latest in equipment and teaching methods for beginners and intermediates. ⓐ La Caleta de Famara ❶ 928 52 86 23 or mobile 686 004 909 (09.00–10.00 and 17.00–18.00) ⓔ info@surfschoollanzarote.com Ⓦ www.surfschoollanzarote.com

Famara Surf ★★
This outfit offers surfing for all levels, with tuition, equipment hire and information on the best places to enjoy north coast surfing to the full, ranging from world-class reef breaks to deserted beach breaks.

@ Avenida El Marinero 39 **t** 928 52 86 76 @ famarasurf@lanzarote.com
w www.famarasurf.com

Walking

Famara makes a good base for keen, independent walkers. The long
beach is a great walk in itself. The top of the Risco de Famara cliffs
provides some thrilling walking with superb views, although care must
be taken in places. Away from the sea, a 10 km (6 mile) track and path
lead from the inland town of Teguise mainly downhill to Famara, again
with excellent views.

EXCURSIONS

Although Famara has an away from it all feeling, Arrecife is just 20 km
(12 miles) away. All the sights of northern Lanzarote can be easily visited
by car from Famara, although it is necessary to go via Teguise (see page
21) because there is little other road access to Famara. Especially within
reach are **Haría** with its 'Valley of 1000 Palms' (see page 77), continuing
to **Mirador del Rio** (see page 78), which is set into the same cliff face
as the **Risco de Famara**, and from **Orzola** (see page 87), an excursion
to **La Graciosa Island** (see page 89). The **Jardín de Cactus** (see page 78)
is also within easy reach, via Teseguite.

It is worthwhile travelling along the little-visited north coast to
La Santa and beyond, and seeing the unvisited, unspoiled coastal scenery
and small fishing and farming communities that survive in this part
of the island.

Club La Santa, at La Santa Sport on the north coast 12 km (7 miles)
west of La Caleta de Famara, is a world-class residential sports resort
with first-class equipment and facilities including an Olympic pool. It
is the setting for international sports and athletics events. Day visitors
are welcome to the resort, but residential stays must be booked well
in advance, through your local agent. UK agents: **Sports Tours Int**
@ 91 Walkden Rd, Walkden, Worsley, Manchester, M28 5DQ, UK
t 0161 790 9890 **f** 0161 790 9811 @ info@clublasanta.co.uk
w www.clublasanta.co.uk

RESTAURANTS

The handful of down-to-earth restaurants near the seafront at La Caleta de Famara are basic but satisfying. They generally offer fresh, locally caught fish and seafood, with typical Canarian dishes such as salted boiled new potatoes with *mojo* sauce.

Las Bajas € This very inexpensive bar/restaurant is a popular spot for a wide range of well-prepared Spanish and international classics. Service and cooking are of a good standard, and credit cards are accepted. ⓐ Avenida Marinero 25, La Caleta de Famara ⓣ 928 52 86 17 ⓛ Open all day Fri–Wed, closed Thurs

A la Bartola € Fish specialities, including locally caught fresh fish of the day, are on the menu at this likeable restaurant where there is live music at weekends. ⓐ Calle Brisa 6, La Caleta de Famara ⓣ 928 52 86 30

Casa Garcia €€ Just a little more expensive than some others, this is a likeable restaurant serving quality fish and seafood specialities, as well as plenty of other dishes, including a variety of paellas. Certainly worth a visit ⓐ Avenida Marinero 1, La Caleta de Famara ⓣ 928 52 87 10

NIGHTLIFE

There is little evening entertainment at the resort other than a leisurely meal or a drink at the low-key restaurants and bars, where the talk at night, as during the day, is mainly of surfing.

Matagorda
the quiet resort

Despite being on the edge of Arrecife Airport – some hotel windows look onto the runway – Matagorda is surprisingly quiet and tranquil, especially in the evenings. The advantage of its location is that the transfer time for arrivals and departures is usually under 15 minutes. This is also the place to find some of the best package holiday bargains, with good modern hotel and self-catering accommodation at modest prices.

The fast national highway skirting Matagorda makes it easy to travel within a few minutes from here into the heart of Puerto del Carmen or Arrecife by car, taxi or on the frequent buses. This gives Matagorda another much-appreciated benefit, that the island's best nightlife, bars and entertainment are readily available, yet Matagorda itself remains peaceful at night.

However, there is no necessity to leave the resort – a single commercial centre provides Matagorda with its own good selection of restaurants, bars and shops. The hotels and self-catering complexes are equipped with swimming pools and sunbathing areas, and put on their own entertainment programmes for both adults and children.

Playa de Matagorda, the resort's narrow beach, forms a pale, sandy sweep around a bright, breezy bay much loved by windsurfing and sailing enthusiasts. At high tide, the sands may in some places be completely covered, leaving the beach compact and damp after the tide withdraws, but the wide promenade provides a pleasant alternative for strolling or sunbathing.

This sunny, airy traffic-free walkway leads all the way into the next bay, **Playa de los Pocillos**, where it joins another promenade following the beach road into neighbouring **Puerto del Carmen**, 4 km (2.5 miles) from Matagorda – the whole distance makes for a manageable and enjoyable walk, with plenty of bars and restaurants along the way if you want to pause for refreshment.

THINGS TO SEE & DO

Cycling ★★★

The fastest and easiest way to travel from Matagorda into Puerto del Carmen, as well as the most enjoyable, is to cycle the 4 km (2.5 miles) on the wide beachside promenade. The biggest bike-hire operation in the area is **MegaFun**, who rent out a large choice of bicycles either by the day or by the week. MegaFun also rent out motorbikes and quad bikes and organize quad bike safaris. ⓐ Playa de los Pocillos ① 928 51 28 93 ⓔ info@megafun-lanzarote.com ⓦ www.megafun-lanzarote.com

Go-karting ★★

The excellent **Gran Karting Club Lanzarote** is a go-karting track for all ages. The senior track allows speeds up to 80 km/h (50 mph), while the junior track (for ages 12–16) gives a chance to try driving at safer speeds. There are mini-karts for the over fives, while children over ten can also try their hand on mini motorcycles called mini-bikes. ⓐ Close to Matagorda, on the main highway just past the Puerto del Carmen turn-off, on La Rinconada, National Highway ① 619 75 99 46 ⓦ www.vista-lanzarote.com/gran_karting/index.html ⓛ Open 10.00–22.00 (summer); 10.00–21.00 (winter)

Rancho Texas Lanzarote ★★★

For an all-American experience, take a trip to Rancho Texas, a theme park built from natural materials such as stone and wood. It is an activity and leisure centre based around horse riding, but there is also plenty of other entertainment, all on a Wild West theme, including lively Country-and-western nights with music, dancing and barbecues. Among the sights are an 'Indian village', 'Medicine Man Cave', 'Goldmine' and a collection of American animals. There are shows with birds of prey, alligators and parrots several times a day. Among the horse-riding options are a three-hour trek for experienced riders and a one-hour trek for beginners. There are also three restaurants on the site .ⓐ Calle Noruega, 35510 Tías ① 928 84 12 86 ⓔ ranchotexas@lanzarote.com ⓦ www.ranchotexaslanzarote.com

SHOPPING

The extensive shopping areas at the heart of Arrecife (see page 14) and Puerto del Carmen (see page 57) are just minutes away by taxi or bus.

Deiland This shopping centre on the main road into Arrecife is much used by locals. Here you will find a good selection of shops selling all kinds of goods, as well as a cafés and bars.

Centro Comercial Matagorda The resort's own pedestrian shopping complex offers a range of souvenirs and beach paraphernalia.

Water sports ★★★

Matagorda is among the best bays on the south coast for windsurfing and sailing. There is equipment hire on the beach for windsurfing and snorkelling, and boat trips for big-game fishing expeditions.

EXCURSIONS

Be sure to take the short trip into Arrecife (see page 14) for all the sightseeing of the island's capital. Organized excursions to Timanfaya and the other sights around the island generally leave from Puerto del Carmen, a few minutes' drive away by bus or taxi, or your tour operator may provide a bus pick-up.

⬥ *Playa de Matagorda*

RESTAURANTS

There are several bars and eating places in the Matagorda commercial centre, including Chinese, Italian, Indian and British ones. For a much bigger choice of restaurants, take a bus or taxi into nearby Arrecife (see page 19) or Puerto del Carmen (see page 62).

Steve's Balti € With a very British atmosphere, apart from the outdoor tables, Steve's restaurant, more of a balti house, in Matagorda commercial centre serves an extensive menu of tasty, typical balti cuisine, including plenty of seafood, meat and vegetarian dishes. There is also a full takeaway service with free delivery within the resort. ⓐ Centro Comercial Matagorda ❶ 928 51 09 87 ⓦ www.stevesbaltihouse.golanzarote.com

NIGHTLIFE

Matagorda's nightlife is fairly low key. Hotels and accommodation complexes put on entertainment or stage shows several evenings a week. There is a small selection of pubs and bars in the Matagorda commercial centre.

Bar Rockola €

Among the bars in the Matagorda commercial centre, Bar Rockola plays popular music of the 50s, 60s and 70s, country-and-western, and rock and roll. A giant screen shows the latest top sporting events. Wines and cocktails, teas and coffees, are served all day. ⓐ Centro Comercial Matagorda ❶ 636 13 54 37 ❷ Open all day until late

The New Inn €

Describing itself as a traditional family pub, this convivial establishment in Matagorda commercial centre offers an extremely full range of entertainment for a pleasant evening out, including disco and karaoke, six TV screens for sports enthusiasts, quizzes and other games and a wide range of drinks. ⓐ Centro Comercial Matagorda ❶ 686 97 03 21 ❷ Open Mon–Fri 17.00 until late, Sat–Sun 13.00 until late

Playa Blanca
south-coast suntrap

The southern coastline of Lanzarote forms a huge, gently curving, sheltered bay, reaching 9 km (5 miles) across from **Pechiguera Point** in the west to **Papagayo Point** in the east. This in turn is divided into three smaller bays, each of which has a sandy beach and rocky outcrops. At the centre of this coast, and rapidly spreading in both directions, lies Lanzarote's third resort.

Playa Blanca occupies a sunny, sheltered position with exquisite, ever-changing views across shimmering blue water towards neighbouring Fuerteventura and, in front of it, tiny Lobos Island.

The focal point of Playa Blanca remains the picturesque former fishing village at its western end, with its alleys and paved lanes. Arguably, though, the resort's greatest attraction is the pedestrianized promenade beside sandy beaches.

Set back from the waterfront are some of the most comfortable and architecturally pleasing modern hotels on the island, which show the potential of imaginative designers who work within the guidelines laid down by César Manrique. Many are almost self-contained, with their own shops, restaurants, pools, sunbathing areas and direct beach access.

In addition, Lanzarote's most southerly resort has a quietly civilized atmosphere, with a privileged and relaxed air, good water sports' facilities and better-than-average restaurants. Because the island's other three big towns are so close to each other, Playa Blanca also has something of a remote feeling about it, even though it is just a 30-minute drive from Puerto del Carmen.

The port itself, with ferries to other islands, remains a vibrant feature of the town. At the other end of town, the latest waterside amenity is an attractive pleasure harbour, **Marina Rubicon** with 400 berths, where luxury yachts are moored.

There are good beaches in the centre of Playa Blanca, but dedicated seekers of sun and sand head out of town on the rough roads to several bigger and better stretches nearby, especially **Papagayo** to the east.

La Perla

Los Calamares

LAS BREÑAS

EL PUESTITO

GALANA

CASTILLO D
COLOF
PLAYA PAPA

AVENIDA PAGAYO

Las Brisas

Las Margaritas

Las Casitas

Casas del Sol

EL CORREILLO

LIMONES

2 **1** Playa Blanca

MAF
RUB

Playa Dorada

3

Puerto de Playa Blanca

4

FERRY TO FUERTEVENTURA

OLD PORT

PUERTO CHICO

Playa Flamingo

N

0 150 300m
0 150 300yds

ATLANTIC OCEAN

THINGS TO SEE & DO

Castillo de las Coloradas ★

Projecting from the Punta del Águila headland just east of Playa Blanca, this fine circular watchtower was first built in 1769 as a lookout to help protect Lanzarote from raiders and pirates. Reconstructed in 1778, its main role today is to give wonderful views across to Fuerteventura.

🕒 Always open ❶ Free access

Marina Rubicón ★★

Opened in 2003 on the Papagayo side of Playa Blanca, Marina Rubicon has already become among the Canaries' most prestigious moorings. The area preserves a traditional architectural style, and there are a number of restaurants, bars and boutiques. ❸ Puerto Deportivo Marina Rubicón, Urbanización Castillo del Águila ❶ 928 51 90 12 ❿ www.marinarubicon.com.

Boat trips ★★★

Leisure cruises from Playa Blanca leave several times a day, including outings to Papagayo beach as well as catamaran excursions, a child-oriented Pirate Cruise and the schooner *Errotea* (❶ 928 517 63 ❸ mareaerrota@retemail.es) and deep-sea fishing excursions. One of the most rewarding is the spectacular trip in the **Yellow Submarine** (❶ 928 51 28 98 ❸ info@submarinesafaris.com), descending to 30 m (98 ft), with windows looking out onto fascinating wrecks and marine life. The price is around €50. Ask your rep for details.

Diving ★★

The **Marina Rubicón Diving Centre** offers daily diving trips to more than 30 exclusive dive sites, including the islands of Lobos and Fuerteventura, plus 'Learn to Dive' courses of 3–5 days duration. ❸ Puerto Deportivo Marina Rubicón ❶ 928 34 93 46 ❸ info@rubicondiving.com ❿ www.rubicondiving.com

Dive College Lanzarote (ⓐ Centro Comercial, La Mulata 1, Montana Roja, Playa Blanca ☎ 606 85 31 09 ⓦ www.scubalanzarote.co.uk) is a leading dive centre running underwater excursions to discover wrecks, caverns and reefs, as well as astonishing marine life such as rays, scorpion fish and angel sharks. It also offers a wide range of PADI courses from beginner to instructor level.

In modern, well-equipped premises 50 m (55 yd) from Playa Dorada beach is **Cala Blanca Diving Centre** founded by Spanish professionals and providing a diverse choice of diving trips,with qualified guides, as well as diving courses for all levels. ⓐ Centro Comercial Papagayo ☎ 928 51 90 40 ☎ Mobile: 607 30 12 30 ⓦ www.calablancasub.com

Stroll the promenade ★★★

Playa Blanca's attractive beachside promenade extends along the whole distance from the Old Port in the west of the resort to the Marina Rubicón in the east. After dark, the lights of Corralejo, in Fuerteventura, can be seen on the horizon.

Visit the Old Port ★★

Not only ferries and pleasure cruises come and go at the bustling port – working fisherman use it too. Watch as they bring in their catch on the quayside, then sample it in the nearby restaurants which overlook the harbour.

🔺 *Colourful boats in the Old Port*

Take a walk ★

Southern Lanzarote is great country for keen walkers. From Playa Blanca there are scenic, easily followed coastal paths to the Pechiguera lighthouse in the west, and Papagayo in the east, both about 5 km (3 miles) away (allow an hour each way and take plenty of water).

BEACHES

Playa Blanca ★★

The name of the town means 'white beach', but the sands of the sheltered town centre bay are golden in colour. The beach is safe for swimming, backed by an attractive promenade, and has been awarded an EU Blue Flag for cleanliness.

Playa Flamingo ★

This is one of the fine sandy bays, safe for swimming, beyond the harbour west of the town. A promenade links the beach to the harbour.

Playa Dorada ★★

In the first bay east of the town centre, this is Playa Blanca's second beach. An EU Blue Flag winner, it is an attractive curve of gently shelving golden sand in a sheltered sun-trap position. Behind is a beach bar where you can hire parasols and sunloungers.

Playa Papagayo ★★

Reached along a bumpy track (or, preferably, by boat from the harbour), the wide, beautiful unspoiled sands of Playa de Papagayo lie about 5 km (3 miles) east of town beyond Castillo de las Coloradas. Considered among Spain's best beaches, it remains undeveloped, despite being a popular haunt for sun-seeking day trippers. There are several other more secluded sandy bays to either side of Papagayo Point, including the favourite for nude sunbathing, **Playa de Puerto Muelas**. There is a simple beach bar at Playa Papagayo, but no other facilities, so take plenty of drinks and food.

EXCURSIONS
Femés village ★

The village church at this quiet inland hill village near Playa Blanca was the first cathedral in the whole of the Canary Islands. Serious walkers can climb from the village to the panoramic Atalaya de Femés for views of Timanfaya in one direction and Fuerteventura in the other.

Fuerteventura ★ ★ ★

Ferries run by the Fred Olsen Line (❶ 928 53 50 90) travel between Playa Blanca and **Corralejo** several times daily. The trip across the 11 km (7 mile) channel between the two islands takes 40 minutes. Alternatively take a full-day inclusive excursion on, for example, the *Cesar II*, which includes bathing platforms and a lunch on board, allows two hours ashore at Corralejo and also takes in a trip to the island of Lobos. ❸ *Cesar II* office at the harbour ❶ 928 81 36 08 ❹ Excursions Mon–Fri ❶ Adults €43 each, children €23

● *Taking a stroll along the beach promenade at Playa Blanca*

SHOPPING

 Town shops There are a few supermarkets and boutiques along Calle Limones, the pedestrianized main street of Playa Blanca's old village, stocking a variety of familiar branded goods. In addition, near the harbour there is a choice of discounted electrical and photographic stores, where it is wise – as in other resorts – to be suspicious of the apparent bargains.

Market Playa Blanca has a small market each Wednesday and Saturday morning in the old village.

Grand Tour ★★★

Offered by most inclusive holiday operators to Playa Blanca, and also available from local travel agencies, the Grand Tour is a day-long excursion from the resort to several of Lanzarote's major sights. Included are the **Timanfaya** volcano drive, a tasting at **La Geria** winery, a trip to **Jameos del Agua** (see page 85), and a lunch stop.

Parque Nacional de Timanfaya ★★★

Playa Blanca is well placed for the sights of western Lanzarote, including **Yaiza** (see page 66) and **Timanfaya** (see page 79), just a 20-minute drive away.

RESTAURANTS & BARS

There is a selection of relaxed cafés and bars serving food all day along the promenade close to the harbour, on the beachside walkway and around the marina. Standards are generally high but check first if you want to pay by credit card.

 El Almacén de la Sal €€€ ❶ A converted salt store provides a cool stone and timber setting for this restaurant, with the best of fresh fish and meat dishes, including international, Spanish and Canarian specialities. Shaded terrace outside, and sometimes live music. ⓐ Avenida Maritima 20 ☎ 928 51 78 85 ⓦ www.almacendelasal.com ⏰ Open for lunch and dinner (snacks all day), closed Tues

🍴 **Brisa Marina** €€ ❷ On the promenade close to the old village and harbour, this restaurant is much liked for its excellent fresh fish and seafood dishes, including both international classics and Canarian specialities. ⓐ Paseo Maritimo 24 ☎ 928 51 72 06 ⏰ Open for lunch and dinner

🍴 **La Cocina del Mar** €€ ❸ With outdoor tables on the promenade near the harbour, and right beside the old village, this seafront restaurant is well positioned. A wide-ranging menu, featuring Italian and other fare, should be able to satisfy all tastes. ⓐ Avenida Maritima 3 ☎ 928 51 86 02 ⏰ Open all day

🍴 **Romantica Grill** €€ ❹ A long-established Playa Blanca restaurant in the old village, the Romantica is popular for a fine array of well-prepared meat dishes in French and Spanish style, such as sirloin steak with Roquefort sauce. There are plenty of other choices too, with fish dishes including perch in lobster sauce. On the menu every Friday night is the islanders' favourite, suckling pig. Good wine list. ⓐ Calle Limones 6 ☎ 928 51 71 66 ⏰ Open for lunch and dinner

NIGHTLIFE

The promenade in Playa Blanca is the heart of evening activity, mainly consisting of restaurants and convivial bars. The hotels have comfortable bars, sometimes with easy-listening live music. After dinner, many of the hotels and self-catering complexes offer stage shows, typically along the lines of Russian dancers, magic shows and tribute bands. Central Playa Blanca becomes quiet at night and is not the right choice for anyone who wants to dance until breakfast time, although there is a disco at **Punta Limones**, west of the resort centre. The nearest all-night music and dance venues are 30 km (19 miles) away in **Puerto del Carmen**.

Playa de los Pocillos
peaceful family resort

The huge, sandy sweep of Pocillos bay is one of the best beaches on the island. At high tide it is largely covered with water, leaving it damp for a while when the tide pulls back – hence its name (pronounced 'pothiyoss'), which means puddle beach. However, it quickly dries again in the warm breeze that blows onto this shore, making it a haven for windsurfers as well as sunbathers.

Pocillos lies just beyond the eastern end of the island's main resort, Puerto del Carmen. It has become a quiet suburb of its livelier, larger neighbour, which is easily accessible on foot (about 20 minutes) on the waterside pavement, or by taxi (about €3). In the other direction, a pleasant beachside promenade runs round to Matagorda in the next bay.

Among the wide range of hotel and self-catering accommodation choices at **Playa de los Pocillos**, most are of a good standard and excellent value for money. Many villas set back from the sea are second homes belonging to prosperous Spanish owners from the mainland. The area is popular with families with young children, and those seeking a peaceful alternative to the more hectic Puerto del Carmen – while still being within walking distance of all its amenities.

There is no need, however, to depend on Puerto del Carmen. At the centre of the Pocillos beachside development, the **Costa Mar** commercial centre has a selection of shops and restaurants. It also has a disco and a couple of bars. At the northern end of the beach, the more upmarket commercial centre **Los Jameos Playa** is an attractive row of shops and high-quality restaurants.

THINGS TO SEE & DO
Quad-biking ★★

Among Lanzarote's top names for hire of quad bikes, Pocillos-based **MegaFun Bikes** also run day trips and safaris all over the island. ⓐ Centro Comercial Costa Mar ⓣ 928 51 28 93 ⓔ info@megafun-lanzarote.com

Windsurfing ★★
If you have your own equipment, bring it to Playa de los Pocillos. If not, there is board rental from beach outlets here or at Puerto del Carmen.

Rancho Texas ★★
An activity and leisure centre with entertainment on a Wild West theme (see page 36) ❸ Calle Noruega, near Playa de los Pocillos ☎ 928 84 12 86 ✉ ranchotexas@lanzarote.com ⒲ www.ranchotexaslanzarote.com

RESTAURANTS

🍴 **Casa Carmen** € An inexpensive little place opposite the Hotel San Antonio, this restaurant serves a wide range of dishes including chicken fajita and Mexican dishes. ❸ Centro Comercial Costa Luz, Avenida de las Playas ☎ 928 51 23 29 ⏱ Open for lunch and dinner

🍴 **Italia Bella** € Italian pizzas and pastas are well made and properly served, with good children's options and reasonable prices. ❸ Centro Comercial Los Jameos Playa ☎ 928 51 47 98 ⏱ Open 09.00–23.00

◉ **O Bota Fumeiro** €€€ In the Costa Luz centre, this first-class seafood restaurant is more French than Spanish in style. Try excellent *calamares*, or sample the steak *al roquefort*. Private parking. ❸ Calle Alemania 9 ☎ 928 51 15 03 ✉ botafumeiro2308@hotmail.com ⏱ Open noon–16.30 and 19.00–midnight, closed Mon

🍴 **Pizzeria Italica** €€ For tasty classic Italian dishes, including charcoal-oven pizza and tasty pasta, this authentic and atmospheric restaurant has a friendly atmosphere and modest prices. ❸ Centro Comercial, Los Jameos Playa ☎ 928 51 16 66 ⏱ Open all day

NIGHTLIFE
Playa de los Pocillos hotels put on their own nightly programmes of stage shows and live music. For a wide range of bars and late-night dance venues, it is just a few minutes on foot or by taxi into Puerto del Carmen.

Playa Quemada
connoisseur's choice

It is a testimony to Lanzarote's lack of rampant development that there are still south-coast waterfront villages that have not yet been taken over by tourism. Playa Quemada (pronounced 'kemarda'), reached by a 4 km (2.5 mile) road from the Tias highway, remains virtually undiscovered.

Due partly to its off-the-beaten track position, Playa Quemada remains a small and simple traditional fishing village of attractive low, white houses, giving a fascinating insight into the Lanzarote of some decades ago. Lying in a calm and sheltered sunny bay protected from strong winds or currents, its seafront, situated beyond the houses, is a beach of dark volcanic rock and stones. Fishermen's boats are moored here.

Although this perhaps makes a poor comparison with the pale sands of the other resorts, it shelves gently into the calm waters and is excellent for swimming. The greatest advantage is the absence of crowds of holidaymakers, except for a few, mainly Spanish, aficionados.

🔽 *The dark volcanic stones of Playa Quemada*

who have discovered this secret place. A better beach can be reached by a short walk over the cliffs or, at low tide, along the shore.

There are, however, a few caravans, as well as several upmarket second homes and holiday villas here, enjoying spectacular ocean views towards the neighbouring islands, **Lobos** and **Fuerteventura**.

For a relaxing escape into sunshine and the simple life, with nothing but fresh-air outdoor activities to distract you from the sunlounger, Playa Quemada is a real find. For sailing enthusiasts, the village is right next door to the smart marina resort of **Puerto Calero** (11 km/7 miles by road). Yet if you feel the need for shopping, entertainment and nightlife, the island's main resort, **Puerto del Carmen**, is only 15 km (9 miles) away.

It is likely that the secret of Playa Quemeda will soon be discovered.

THINGS TO SEE & DO

Diving ★★

Based in nearby Puerto Calero, the Dive Centre run by **Diving Lanzarote** is highly respected for its varied and professional dives under the care of highly qualified instructors. Among the dives on offer are trips to Playa Quemada to explore the Quemada Ledges, diving into shallow or deep water as preferred over a rocky reef. Taking the deeper option (down to 28 m/92 ft), there are ledges where large fish such as angel sharks and stingrays can be seen, as well as numerous small fish such as damselfish, wrasse and bream. Quemada Menor is a fascinating, more shallow dive on a smaller reef, where large shoals of sardines, sea cucumbers and barracuda can be seen. The Dive Centre is both a BSAC School and a PADI Dive Centre, offering courses from introductory dives for the absolute beginner up to more advanced courses. ➌ Puerto Calero Marina ➊ 928 51 18 80 ➋ info@divelanzarote.com ➍ www.divelanzarote.com

Horse riding ★★

Lanzarote a Caballo, located on the main highway between the Puerto Calero and Playa Quemada junctions, is an equestrian activity centre offering horse riding for all levels at the site, for exploring the local countryside on horseback or for guided sightseeing tours of the island.

At an entertaining children's park called **Fort Apache**, children can enjoy activities with horses and ponies. The site has its own restaurant, **Lanzarote a Caballo** ⓐ Carretera Arrecife-Yaiza, Km 17 ⓣ 928 83 03 14 or 626 64 73 68 ⓕ 928 81 39 95 ⓔ lanzaroteacaballo@lanzarote.com ⓦ www.lanzaroteacaballo.com

Walking ★★

For exploring the south coast on foot, this is an exceptional area, with fairly well-marked coastal and hill paths. In Playa Quemada, follow the main street uphill and continue out of the village, where the road becomes a track. This leads over the hills on a relatively easy, but thrilling, walk to **Puerto Calero** (see page 52).

BEACHES

Apart from the rocky Playa Quemada seashore, it is possible to follow footpaths around small headlands to reach other bays and beaches. The nearest, **Playa de la Arena**, is a beach of black sand just a few minutes' walk from **Playa Quemada**. It is popular for nude sunbathing.

EXCURSIONS

Playa Quemada is close to the inland volcanic wine growing region **La Geria** (see page 75), the picturesque village of **Yaiza** (see page 66) on the edge of the *malpaís*, and **Parque Nacional de Timanfaya** (see page 79).

RESTAURANTS

Playa Quemada has a handful of tapas bars and a few small restaurants specializing in good fish and seafood at low prices. The nearest wider choice of restaurants is at Puerto Calero (11 km/7 miles away).

La Caravana €€ Enjoy a range of tasty meat dishes in a fascinating setting at the restaurant of the riding and activity centre Lanzarote a Caballo. It is on the main road between the Playa Quemada and Puerto Calero junctions. ⓐ Carretera Arrecife-Yaiza, Km 17 ⓣ 928 83 00 38 ⓛ Open 10.00–18.00

Puerto Calero
marina with style

One of Europe's most prestigious yacht marinas clings to the rocky coast south of Puerto del Carmen. It displays to the full the appeal of Lanzarote to a chic, well-to-do crowd, including many wealthy Spanish families. The harbour has 420 floating wharves capable of berthing boats of from 8 to 75 m (9 to 82 ft) in length, and a ravishing selection of luxury craft can often be seen moored here. To add to the scene, dark hills rise steeply behind, and huge shoals of bright fish swim among the yachts floating in the perfectly clear waters.

Puerto Calero has quickly established itself as one of Europe's most beautiful marinas. It occupies a magnificent setting, literally blasted out of the dark rocks of this glorious stretch of coastline, and has the appeal to yachtsmen of a safe berth for Atlantic sailing in African latitudes. Although Lanzarote's best-known artist was César Manrique, another of the island's sons is the acclaimed modern architect Luis Ibanez Margalef. It was Margalef who first conceived and designed this attractive harbour in the 1980s.

However, a dramatic change came a decade later with the decision to double the size of the marina, a project that came to fruition in 2001. Puerto Calero moved from being a sailing paradise to a fully fledged resort, with two luxury hotels and a range of comfortable detached and semi-detached self-catering villas. True to Manrique's guidelines, all the accommodation is in step with the island's traditional architecture and is sensitive to the surrounding environment.

To enjoy Puerto Calero, there is no need to be a keen yachtsman or even to step on board a boat at all. Many day visitors arrive by road, and have come simply to stroll, or to enjoy a lazy lunch at the terrace of one of the many excellent bars and restaurants on the quayside. In addition to the resort's marine activities, there are sports facilities, an art gallery and a museum. Puerto Calero is definitely a place to visit if you enjoy the finer things in life.

THINGS TO SEE & DO

Canarian Cetacean Museum ★★

Cetaceans are the whale and dolphin family. The **Canarian Cetacean Museum (CCM)**, housed inside a former dry dock, offers visitors the chance to discover one of Europe's major cetacean collections. Visitors can experience the Canary Islands' ocean setting and learn about these remarkable creatures through images, sound, full-size replicas and biological exhibits. There is also a gift shop. ☎ 928 84 95 60 928 84 95 61 @ info@museodecetaceos.org W www.museodecetaceos.org ⏰ Open 11.00–19.00 (summer); 10.00–18.00 (winter)

Catamaran excursions ★★★

Treat yourself to a day on board a catamaran with **Catlanza**. The cats sail from the marina along the coast to Playa Blanca and a break at Papagayo beach. Bar service, lunch, snorkelling equipment and a jet-ski ride are all included in the trip. ➌ Puerto Calero marina ☎ 928 51 30 22 @ catlanza@lanzarote.com W www.lanzarote.com/catlanza

Diving ★★★

Puerto Calero's highly professional **Dive Centre** organizes BSAC and PADI courses from introductory dives for the absolute beginner up to advanced, and dives around the island for all abilities. Depending on currents, it is also possible to travel to a small wreck.
➌ Puerto Calero Marina
☎ 928 51 18 80
@ info@divelanzarote.com
W www.divelanzarote.com

🔺 *Puerto Calero's pristine marina*

Fishing excursions ⭑

Keen anglers wanting to try big-game fishing can choose from a number of companies. **Lanzarote Fishing Club**, based at the marina, offer outings in specially designed boats in the care of experienced skipper Tino García. 🅐 Calle Camino del Mesón 49 B 🆃 636 47 40 00 🅕 928 51 43 78 🅔 fishingclub@lanzarote.com

Horse riding ⭑⭑

Discover the area on horseback with **Lanzarote a Caballo**, an equestrian centre about 4 km (2.5 miles) from Puerto Calero. It offers riding tours and activities for all ages and levels, including guided sightseeing tours, and there is a children's section. 🅐 Carretera Arrecife-Yaiza, Km 17 🆃 928 83 03 14 🅔 lanzaroteacaballo@lanzarote.com

Puerto Calero Art Gallery ⭑

The inspiration for this ambitious gallery derives from the principles of César Manrique – to create a harmonious interaction between art, landscape, local culture and the visitor. The museum's aim is to acquire and promote local art and artists. 🅐 Puerto Calero marina 🆃 928 51 15 05 🅔 galeriadearte@puertocalero.com 🕒 Open Tues–Sat 11.00–14.00 and 17.00–21.00, closed Mon

Sailing with a crew ⭑⭑

Sample the good life for a day on a luxury 15 m (50 ft) skippered yacht with professional crew. No previous sailing experience needed. Charter for up to ten people. **Yachtaholic** 🅐 Puerto Calero (UK address: 39 Eltham Road, West Bridgford, Nottingham) 🆃 627 24 55 82 🅔 info@yachtaholic.com 🆆 www.yachtaholic.com

Submarine Safaris ⭑⭑⭑

Come on board the modern 18.5 m (7 ft) long submarine *Sub Fun III* and descend into a magical marine world. The submarine is air conditioned, with air pressure maintained at normal atmospheric levels. A highly professional team provide you with an unforgettable outing. No children

⬥ *Chartering a luxury yacht is a wonderful way to see the area*

under two years. ② Submarine Safaris SL, Puerto Calero marina
① 928 51 28 98 or 928 51 29 06 ⑥ info@submarinesafaris.com
ⓦ www.submarinesafaris.com ⓛ Excursions at 10.00, noon, 14.00, 16:00

Water sports ★
A wide range of other rentals or water sports at the marina include
jet-ski hire and paracraft.

BEACHES
Puerto Calero has no beach of its own, but **Puerto del Carmen** is just
5 km (3 miles) away on the new direct road.

EXCURSIONS
A full range of inclusive sightseeing excursions is offered by the hotels
and self-catering complexes. For independent travellers, **Puerto Calero** is
within easy reach of the inland volcanic wine-growing region **La Geria**
(see page 75), the picturesque village of **Yaiza** (see page 66) on the edge
of the *malpaís*, and **Parque Nacional De Timanfaya** (see page 79).

RESTAURANTS

El Bar del Club €€ This very popular and attractive place to meet friends and relax offers a wide range of well-prepared à la carte international dishes. There are good sea views both from inside and the large terrace. ⓐ Puerto Calero marina ⓣ 928 51 31 81 ⓕ 928 51 14 62 ⓛ Tues–Sun 13.00–23.00

Lani's Grill del Puerto €€ Like the rest of the very popular Lani's chain of resort eateries, this restaurant has a reliable, tasty menu at modest prices. Here the emphasis is on grills. ⓐ Paseo Marítimo ⓣ 928 51 07 03 ⓛ Open approximately 10.00–midnight

McSorley's Irish Bar € This friendly and enjoyable pub serves food and drink all day and into the evening, including familiar beers of home as well as local brews. The menu is British, offering the best of pub food. Nightly entertainment. ⓐ Puerto Calero Marina ⓣ 680 42 46 65 ⓦ www.McSorleysLanzarote.com ⓛ Open from breakfast to late at night

La Pappardella €€ At the far end of the promenade, this is one of Lanzarote's best Italian restaurants. Service is friendly yet efficient and prices very moderate. ⓐ Paseo Marítimo ⓣ 928 51 29 11 ⓛ Open noon–01.00

El Tomate € This pleasant and useful little café has outdoor tables with a view of the boats coming and going. A good spot for a quick snack, *bocadillos* or tapas. ⓐ Calle Teide, Puerto Calero ⓣ 928 51 22 10 ⓛ Open all day

NIGHTLIFE

The marina's restaurants and bars remain open until late in Puerto Calero. For late-night discos and clubs, travel the 5 km (3 miles) into **Puerto del Carmen**.

Puerto del Carmen
the main resort

Lanzarote's principal resort is the focal point for all its energetic youth-oriented nightlife and there is a lively, busy holiday scene during the day, yet even here the island keeps its unique charm. The strict guidelines laid down by artist César Manrique have prevented the building of any high-rise hotels, so Puerto del Carmen retains a delightfully low-key, small-town feel. Most buildings are only two storeys high and have traditional white walls and painted woodwork.

The resort consists of little more than a single long main street, Avenida de las Playas, running right beside the sea. On one side of the Avenida there is a string of enticing open-fronted eateries, bars and shops; the other side is mainly devoted to a delightful flower-decked promenade, alongside landscaped gardens and a vast beach of golden sand.

Where the main beach ends, the promenade continues to a rockier foreshore, a smaller beach and yet more beautiful sea views. At the southern end of the resort, an older district of quaint lanes clusters around the picturesque little port that gives the town its name. The original Old Port survives today as a bustling restaurant district with a good deal of authentic Spanish flavour. The promenade continues north beyond **Puerto del Carmen** into neighbouring **Playa de los Pocillos** and **Matagorda**. The easiest way to get from one beach to the next is on foot or by bicycle, but taxis and frequent buses also connect the three resorts.

🔵 *Lazy days at Puerto del Carmen*

THINGS TO SEE & DO

Old Port ★★★

Where the beach ends, the resort's waterfront becomes a tangled area of old lanes leading to a delightful little former fishing port, the original Puerto del Carmen. There are still fishing boats in the harbour, as well as leisure craft and larger boats, and many strollers by the waterside, all together creating a bustling and enjoyable scene. A string of bars and restaurants, some climbing to terraces with wide views, runs alongside the port.

Puerto Calero ★★★

Be sure to take in a trip – by road or by water or even on a clifftop footpath – to this attractive upmarket marina lying just 5 km (3 miles) away from Puerto del Carmen. It makes an enjoyable outing even if only to sit with a coffee and admire the smart yachts at their moorings. See pages 53–55 for details of the many facilities for water sports, leisure activities and boat excursions available at the marina.

Diving ★★

Diving Lanzarote, based at the Dive Centre in nearby Puerto Calero, is a top name in Canaries diving offering varied and professional dives under the care of highly qualified instructors. They can collect clients from

Puerto del Carmen. Several of the dives on offer are just off the coast of Puerto del Carmen, close to the Hotel Fariones at the southern end of the beach, where dives to depths of between 12 and 35 m (39–115 ft) reveal a fascinating underwater environment. Electric rays, shoals of tuna, stingrays and angel sharks can be seen, and the deeper dive visits a cave which is frequented by groupers. ⓐ Puerto Calero Marina ⓣ 928 51 18 80 ⓔ info@divelanzarote.com ⓦ www.divelanzarote.com

Go-karting ★★

Close to Matagorda, on the main highway just past the Puerto del Carmen turn-off, **Gran Karting Club Lanzarote** is an excellent track for visitors of all ages. The senior track allows speeds up to 80 km/h (50 mph), while the junior track (for ages 12–16) allows for driving at safer speeds. There are mini-karts for the over fives, and children over ten can also try their hand on mini motorcycles. ⓐ La Rinconada, National Highway ⓣ 619 75 99 46 ⓦ www.vista-lanzarote.com ⓒ 10.00–22.00 (summer); 10.00–21.00 (winter)

⊙ *The Old Port at Puerto del Carmen*

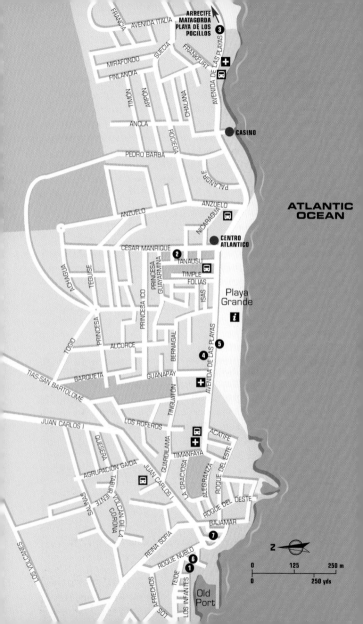

Horse riding ★★

Lanzarote a Caballo offers horse riding for all levels either at the site, or exploring the local countryside on horseback. There is also a fun children's park called Fort Apache, where the kids can enjoy activities with horses and ponies. The site has a good restaurant. ⓐ Located close to Puerto del Carmen on the main highway (just beyond the Puerto Calero junction), Carretera Arrecife-Yaiza, Km 17 ⓣ 928 83 03 14 or 626 4 73 68 ⓕ 34 928 81 39 95 ⓔ lanzaroteacaballo@lanzarote.com ⓦ www.lanzaroteacaballo.com

Cycling ★★

The fastest way to travel from Matagorda into Puerto del Carmen, and the most enjoyable, is to cycle the 4 km (2.5 miles) on the wide beachside promenade. The biggest bike-hire operation in the area is **MegaFun Bikes**, who rent out a large choice of bicycles by the day or by the week. They also rent out motorbikes and quad bikes and organize bike safaris. ⓐ Playa de los Pocillos. ⓣ 928 51 28 93 ⓔ info@megafun-lanzarote.com ⓦ www.megafun-lanzarote.com

Rancho Texas ★★★

Rancho Texas is an activity and leisure centre based on horse riding, but with a lot of other entertainment on a Wild West theme, including lively country-and-western nights with music, dancing and barbecues. Sights include an 'Indian village', 'Medicine Man Cave', 'Goldmine', and a collection of American animals. There are shows with birds of prey and alligators several times daily. Among the horse-riding options are a three-hour trek for experienced riders and a one-hour trek designed for beginners. There are three restaurants on the site. ⓐ Calle Noruega, 35510 Tías ⓣ 928 84 12 86 ⓔ ranchotexas@lanzarote.com ⓦ www.ranchotexaslanzarote.com

Submarine Safaris ★★★

A trip on the submarine Sub Fun III is one of the most popular and enjoyable activities. The modern 18.5 m (22 ft) long vessel is air conditioned, with air pressure maintained at normal atmospheric levels. It descends into a magical underwater world viewed through 22 large windows. A highly professional team provide you with an unforgettable outing. No children under two years of age are permitted. **ⓐ** Submarine Safaris SL, Puerto Calero marina (pick-up from Puerto del Carmen hotels) **ⓣ** 928 51 28 98 or 928 51 29 06 **ⓔ** info@submarinesafaris.com **ⓦ** www.submarinesafaris.com **ⓛ** Excursions 10.00, noon, 14.00 and 16.00

Water sports ★
There is equipment hire on the beach for windsurfing, jet skis and other water sports. Basic tuition is given.

BEACHES
Playa Grande, the very spacious, safe and sandy main beach in the centre of the resort has an EU Blue Flag for cleanliness and water quality. Sunloungers and parasols are for hire.

EXCURSIONS
The resort is ideally placed for touring both in the north and south of the island. Tour operators and local agencies offer half-day and full-day excursions from the resort to all the main sights of the island, especially Lanzarote's number one sight, the beautiful **Parque Nacional de Timanfaya** (see page 79). Early on Sunday mornings, coaches leave Puerto del Carmen for the big weekly craft market in the inland town of **Teguise** (see page 21).

RESTAURANTS (see map on page 60)
For more character and classier cooking (but with higher prices), the Old Port is usually the best choice for a good lunch or dinner. Catering more to simple family dining, the **Avenida de las Playas** is said to have around 200 restaurants along its length. Most display pictures outside of what is on offer, usually familiar favourites like pizza, steak and chips or spaghetti bolognese. Few accept reservations – just choose one you like and take a seat.

El Bodegón €€ ❶ Atmospherically kitted out as a wine cellar of years gone by, this Old Port restaurant serves a selection of tasty tapas and fresh meat grilled at your table. ⓐ Avenida del Varadero ❶ 928 51 11 61 ⓛ Open 12.30–16.00 and 18.30–23.30

La Cañada €€€ ❷ This well-established restaurant off the Avenida is considered one of Lanzarote's best places for fine dining. On the menu is a range of tasty meat, fish and seafood dishes. Air conditioned. ⓐ Calle César Manrique 2–3 ❶ 928 51 04 15 ❶ 928 51 21 08 ⓛ Open Mon–Sun noon–midnight, closed Sun evening

Casa Carmen € ❸ A very inexpensive place in the Costa Luz centre at the Pocillos end of town, this surprisingly small restaurant serves a wide range of dishes, including chicken *fajita* and an unexpected Mexican selection. ⓐ Avenida de las Playas 69 ❶ 928 51 23 29 ⓛ Open for lunch and dinner

Lani's €€ ❹ A popular local chain with several different branches along the Avenida, each serves a different style of cooking. Among them are Lani's Bistro, Lani's Café, Lani's Grill, Lani's Pizza and Lani's Terraza. All are relaxed and bustling, and serve good food at a moderate price. ⓐ Avenida de las Playas ⓛ Open 10.00–midnight

El Mirador € ❺ One of the only bar-restaurants on the beach side of the Avenida. A perfect spot to enjoy a drink or lunch with a wonderful sea view. ⓐ Opposite Centro Comercial Arena Dorada, Avenida de las Playas ⓛ Open all day

El Puerto Viejo €€€ ❻ Top dining in the Old Port area at this grill restaurant, whose acclaimed chef Luis León Romero uses the best and freshest of local ingredients to make a range of international and local specialities. Good sea views and decor is on an appropriately maritime theme. ⓐ Avenida del Varadero ❶ 928 51 52 65 ⓔ puertoviejo@lanzarote.com ⓛ Open 12.30–16.00 and 18.30–23.30

El Sardinero €€€ **➐** Among the most highly praised fish restaurants in Puerto del Carmen, this relaxed, unpretentious and informal place is in the port area at the west end of the seafront (but with little or no sea view). Choose grilled sardines or *sancocho*, for example, or you can just point out the fish you want – come early for a good choice. **ⓐ** Calle Nuestra Señora del Carmen 9 **ⓣ** 928 51 18 47 **ⓔ** personal@casatinosardinero.com **ⓦ** www.casatinosardinero.com **ⓛ** Open 10.00–00.30

NIGHTLIFE

After dark, Avenida de las Playas becomes Lanzarote's busiest entertainment district. The focal point is the **Centro Atlantico**, about halfway along the avenue. Here, there is something for many different tastes and budgets, ranging from convivial pubs and cocktails bars to cabaret venues, nightclubs and all-night dance clubs.

Casino

Play the slot machines during the day at the Casino, or dress up and come at night to gamble your holiday money in its gaming rooms where roulette tables, ruleta and blackjack are played. There is a restaurant, bar and cabaret entertainment. The casino is not glamorous, but all guests must be over 18, appropriately dressed and in possession of a passport. **ⓐ** Centro Ocio, Avenida de las Playas 12 **ⓣ** 928 51 50 00 **ⓕ** 928 51 50 69 **ⓦ** www.casinodelanzarote.com **ⓛ** Slot machines 11.00–16.00; bar and game hall 10.00–04.00; restaurant 21.00–02.00

Clubs & discos

Late-night music and dance venues cluster around the Atlantico strip. Each appeals to its own crowd, though many clubbers drift from one to another. Among top names in this area are **Atomic Revolution**, **Big Apple, Caesars, Dreams, Harley Rock Diner and Disco, Hippodrome, Ibiza, Papagayo, Paradise, Tequila Bar** and **Tropical**. **ⓛ** Opening hours are generally 10.00–05.00, with most places remaining fairly quiet before midnight.

🔺 *Beautiful sunsets on the water*

Cocktail bars

Catering to a more grown-up crowd, several attractive bars offer snacks and meals in the early evening followed by dancing into the small hours. Exotic cocktails are the speciality. The longest established, the **Waikiki Beach Club** has a large terrace upstairs and a downstairs with disco or live music. 🅐 Centro Comercial Atlantico 🅦 www.waikiki-beach-club.com

Pubs & bars

Several big bars with screens and entertainment stay open until late. One of the popular Irish bars, has music ranging from traditional Irish to current hits, singalongs, drinks specials, and the latest sports events on giant screens. **O'Donoghues** 🅐 Centro Comercial Atlantico 🅦 www.odonoghues-lanzarote.com 🅛 Open 21.30–04.00. Other bars are on an English or Scottish theme. In the Old Port area **Cervecería San Miguel** has a more Spanish flavour, with music and screens and good food. 🅐 Avenida del Varadero 🅛 Open 10.00–03.00

Shows

Erotic floor shows and striptease are offered by some nightclubs, such as **Curva**, **Club Venus** and **Top Cats**. More comic performances, especially drag shows, feature at **Lady Muck** 🅐 Calle Cesar Manrique, or at one of the resort's most popular venues, **Titti Trollop's Music Tavern** 🅐 Centro Comercial La Penita 🅐 Avenida de las Playas 🅦 www.tittitrollop.co.uk

Yaiza
the prettiest village

More than once this extraordinary, tranquil little village in the very south of Lanzarote has won the contest to find the 'Most Beautiful Village' in Spain. Its simple, traditional white houses, small and unpretentious, form an oasis of light and a stunning contrast to the starkness of the volcanic environment that creeps to its very edges.

In the other direction, away from the volcano which looms so close, the town looks towards the sunburnt farmland that surrounded it completely until 1730. This is when Timanfaya began the six-year eruption that by the end had destroyed half of Yaiza's farms and most its houses. The villagers first of all fled for their lives, then made their way back to their desolate homes to rebuild what they could.

Today, it is hard to believe that such hardship ever happened. With dazzling white walls, sometimes charmingly adorned with balconies or flowers, palm trees or gardens, Yaiza's handsome little houses look well ordered and comfortable. The village became the inspiration for César Manrique, who eventually established architectural rules to help the whole of Lanzarote preserve this simple traditional appearance.

Inevitably, Yaiza has since become a magnet for visitors. Manrique would not have minded that – he expected it, which is why he restored an old Yaiza farmhouse as a stylish restaurant, La Era. On the edge of the village, a couple of traditional old country houses have been turned into smart little hotels of character. Several of the village houses have become elegant self-catering accommodation.

Yaiza makes a perfect base for exploring the national park, for visiting Timanfaya before the tour buses have arrived from the other resorts, or after they have left again, and for imbibing the atmosphere of the lonely *malpaís*. It is also well placed for visits to all the other sights of western and southern Lanzarote, and despite its inland situation, is only a short drive from resorts and sandy beaches such as **Playa Blanca** and **Puerto del Carmen**.

🔺 *Enjoy a camel ride up to the top of Timanfaya*

THINGS TO SEE & DO
Camel rides ★★

Yaiza is believed to be the only place in the world with a specially constructed underpass so that camels can cross the road. In fact, Lanzarote's 'camels' are dromedaries. If you would like to ride one of them in the *malpaís* or up to the top of Timanfaya, call in at the **Echadero de los Camellos** (Camel Park), 3 km (2 miles) north of Yaiza.
ⓐ Parque Nacional de Timanfaya road ● Open 09.00–16.00

Horse riding ★★

Horse-back tours of the area begin just 4 km (2.5 miles) away from Yaiza at **Lanzarote a Caballo**, an equestrian centre offering riding tours and activities for all ages and all levels, including guided sightseeing tours. There is a children's section called **Fort Apache**. ⓐ Carretera Arrecife-Yaiza, Km 17 ⓣ 928 83 03 14 ⓔ lanzaroteacaballo@lanzarote.com

La Era ★★★

Set back from the main through road, and clearly signposted, La Era is not just a restaurant, but a historical sight well worth seeing even without having a meal. A 300-year-old farmhouse with outbuildings, La Era is unusual in having survived the 18th-century volcanic eruptions. The buildings were restored by César Manrique. The traditional green outer doorway leads into the main courtyard and gardens, off which the former farm buildings now house today's dining rooms (see page 70), bar and shop. ⓐ Carretera General, Yaiza ⓣ 928 83 00 16 ⓛ Open for visitors as well as diners, 11.00–16.00 and 19.00–23.00

Village centre ★★★

The centre of the village has an arty, civilized atmosphere. There is a municipal art gallery in the **Casa de Cultura** (signposted in the village), while the **Galería Yaiza** art gallery (also signposted in the village) displays local painting and ceramic work, most of which is offered for sale. In the main square, Plaza de los Remedios, step inside the cool 18th-century village church.

BEACHES

Yaiza is only 15–20 minutes drive from the sandy beaches of two resorts. **Puerto del Carmen** (see page 57) offers a lively atmosphere and plenty of seafront facilities. Or for a quieter, family setting and a choice of good, sandy beaches with safe bathing, choose **Playa Blanca** (see page 39).

EXCURSIONS
Volcanic landscapes ★★

The volcanic *malpaís* starts at the edge of the village, with the border of the Parque Nacional de Timanfaya just 8 km (5 miles) away. At the heart of the national park, Mount Timanfaya itself, and the coach tour of the

Montanas del Fuego (Mountains of Fire) which surround it, is a must (see page 79). Only 4 km (2.5 miles) from Yaiza (via Uga) are the volcanic vineyards of **La Geria** (see page 75).

Fuerteventura and Lobos Island ★★★

Under 20 minutes away, on the fast road across the flatlands south of Yaiza, is the port of **Playa Blanca**, from which ferries and excursions leave several times daily for the neighbouring island of Fuerteventura and the smaller Lobos Island (see page 94).

Plaza de los Remedios

RESTAURANTS

El Campo €€ A good, unpretentious establishment near the village football pitch, this is the locals' top choice for a range of popular local and international dishes like fresh fish and meat stew and pizzas. ❸ Football ground (signposted) ❶ 928 83 03 44 ❶ Open 09.00–23.00

La Era €€ Inside this restored farmhouse, the attractively laid tables are set out in a group of small rooms. Service is professional and helpful, and the menu focuses strongly on the best of Canarian specialities, such as meaty stews, grilled goat's cheese and *papas arrugadas*. To go with it, try a bottle of La Era's own crisp, tasty white wine. Desserts are rich, sweet local concoctions (see also page 68). ❸ Carretera General, Yaiza ❶ 928 83 00 16 ❶ Open 11.00–16.00 and 19.00–23.00

NIGHTLIFE

Beyond a leisurely dinner and a stroll under the stars, there is little nightlife in Yaiza itself. The neighbouring village of **Uga** has a bar with karaoke. For a big selection of late-night bars, pubs and clubs, take a taxi into nearby **Puerto del Carmen** (see page 57).

EXCURSIONS
Out & about

Southern Tour
day trip from Puerto del Carmen

There is an intimate, rustic feel to much of the southern half of the island. Despite containing the malpaís which consumed so much of their farmland, this remains the Lanzarote of the country people, where their traditions and culture are most accessible. Take the main exit road from Puerto del Carmen, and on reaching the round-about at the edge of town, cross straight over to continue via Tias and San Bartolomé towards Mozaga.

THE TOUR
Monumento al Campesino (Monument to the Countryman) ★★

At the junction outside the wine village of Mozaga stands César Manrique's curious sculpture dedicated to the *campesino* – the long-suffering farming man on whose labours, he believed, the whole of society rests. The extraordinary monument, in a cubist form, has been created from an assemblage of discarded fragments of farm and fishing implements, water tanks and fishing boats, and depicts a farmer with his animals. To emphasize the honour due to such country people, Manrique has placed his unusual monument at the very centre of the island.

La Casa Museo del Campesino
(The Countryman's House Museum) ★★

Alongside the Campesino Monument is another work by Manrique dedicated to Lanzarote's farming people, the Casa Museo del Campesino. This is a replica of a traditional simple farmhouse and farmyard, as perfect and beautiful as a piece of art rather than as domestic architecture. Inside are the rooms and equipment of a typical country dwelling of some decades ago, as well as workshops where traditional craftsmen can be seen at their work. Their products are on sale in the museum's craft shop, and there is also a good, inexpensive country-style restaurant serving classic local dishes. ☎ 928 52 01 36 ⏱ Museum 10.00–18.00; restaurant 12.30–16.30

🔺 *César Manrique's sculpture*

Mozaga ⭐

Straight ahead, Mozaga is an authentic, attractive unspoiled wine village. It has good *bodegas* where you can buy local wines. On the edge of the village, Caserío de Mozaga is a luxury small hotel and restaurant of character, which is housed in a beautifully restored 18th-century country house.

Museo Agricola el Patio (El Patio Agricultural Museum) ★★

Continue from Mozaga to rustic Tiagua, where the Agricultural Museum is a restored traditional farm acting as a vivid record of local life a century ago. Guides take you to see the farm's restored windmills, a cactus garden, fascinating, eclectic displays on local arts, crafts and architecture and a permanent exhibition of old photographs. After the tour, wine tasting is available, and there is a small bar. ☎ 928 52 91 06 🕐 Open Mon–Fri 10.00–17.30, Sat 10.00–14.30, closed Sun

Ermita de los Dolores (Hermitage of Our Lady of Sorrows) ★

The Tinguaton road leads across open country and, on the edge of the village of Tinguaton, reaches a big church of jet-black volcanic stones outlined in white. This is the Hermitage of Notre Dame de los Dolores (Our Lady of Sorrows), the focal point for the island's biggest annual religious celebration, the Fiesta de la Virgen de los Volcanes on 15 September, when local people honour the Virgin for saving them from destruction during the volcanic eruption of 1824. Inside is the statue of the Virgin, the much-revered Virgen de los Volcanes (Virgin of the Volcanoes), which is carried in procession at the fiesta. There is a simple bar/restaurant opposite the church.

Parque Nacional de Timanfaya ★★★

The road begins to cross black and grey volcanic terrain and enters the volcanic area of the Parque Nacional de Timanfaya (see page 79).

El Golfo ★

Reaching the national highway, bypass Yaiza and take the right turn for El Golfo, on the brutally volcanic west coast. Here the pounding Atlantic has eroded a half-submerged volcanic cone into an exquisite emerald-coloured lagoon amid a backdrop of colour-streaked cliffs.

To go down to the lagoon, look for the small road (signposted) 2 km (1 mile) before El Golfo village, and follow the footpath. The village of El Golfo is acclaimed for its restaurants preparing excellent fresh fish and shellfish.

Salinas de Janubio (Janubio saltpans) ★

Some 8 km (5 miles) south along the desolate coast is the lagoon that has become the angular, geometric Janubio saltpans. Salt production has long been an important feature of the island economy, for use in fish preservation. All around the Lanzarote coast, there are small saltpans. Janubio is the oldest and still the most productive.

Yaiza ★★

Continue on the road 8 km (5 miles) back into Yaiza (see page 67). **Restaurante La Era** in the village makes a good place for lunch.

Uga ★

Pretty Uga consists of simple and traditional small white houses. This wine village has plenty of greenery and provides a sharp contrast to the volcanic landscapes that lie nearby. Apart from wine, Uga is known for its camel (dromedary) breeders. **Restaurante Gregorio** (€€) is the village inn, serving local specialities (closed Tuesday).

La Geria Valley ★★★

Leaving Uga, turn left onto the La Geria Valley road, which quickly enters a strange landscape of broken grey *malpaís* where grapes are cultivated. Beside the road – narrow and difficult driving in places – are vine bushes that produce Lanzarote's best crisp white malvasia wine. Each vine bush nestles in its own separate hollow, individually protected by a horseshoe of piled-up lava rocks. It all looks more like art than agriculture. As you pass one of the occasional roadside *bodegas*, stop by to taste, and maybe buy, some of the wine they produce. After some 10 km (6 miles) the road passes the oldest *bodega* in the Canaries, **El Grifo**, still a leading name.

Mácher ★

Turn back to the Mácher turning (7.5 km/5 miles from Uga), which leads over a hill to the small community of Mácher, where several upmarket holiday villas look down towards the sea. Continue across the main road back into Puerto del Carmen.

Northern Tour
day trip from Arrecife

The northern half of the island includes quiet agricultural landscapes, surprisingly green and gentle in places, with few signs of the volcanic presence – except for the layer of black picón, black pebbles of volcanic rock sprinkled onto fields to hold moisture and make it more productive. Along the way are unspoilt villages and towns, and several unmissable sights. Avoid following this route on a Sunday, the one day when the road may be busy. Leave Arrecife on the main Tahiche and Teguise road.

◗ *The incredible Cactus Garden*

THE TOUR
Fundación César Manrique ★★★
Arriving at Tahiche, note the remarkable mobile sculpture standing at
the roundabout just before the town. This is one of the many mobiles
César Manrique erected around the island. Turn left here to arrive at his
former home, now the Fundación César Manrique (see page 83).

Teguise ★★
Passing through pleasant rolling country, and skirting the popular
self-catering villa development at Nazaret, the road reaches Teguise, the
island's historic former capital (see page 88).

Castillo de Santa Barbara (Santa Barbara Castle) ★
On the hill of Guanapay beside Teguise, this handsome 14th-century
fortress of pale stone was first built in the 14th century by Lancelloti
Malocello to guard against Arab pirates. Most of the existing building –
also known as Castillo de Guanapay – dates from the 16th century. Now
as then, it gives wide views.

The castle houses the **Museo del Emigrante Canario**, a fascinating
museum about the emigration of Canary Islanders to the Americas. After
the volcanic eruptions of the 18th and 19th centuries, a large proportion
of Lanzarote's population fled to Venezuela.

Reached via a signposted track on the other side of the main road as
it bypasses Teguise. ☎ 928 81 19 50 ☉ Open 10.00–15.00, closed Mon

Haría ★★
Follow the road as it climbs on the way to Haría. Along the way are some
fine viewpoints. A left turn signed to **Ermita de las Nieves** leads up to a
small white chapel with panoramic views. The **Mirador de Haría**, just
before the town, gives a superb view over the **Valley of 1000 Palms**, the
town almost hidden by the many trees growing in this valley of fields
and flowers. Tranquil Haría, with its picturesque narrow streets and
squares, white walls and brightly coloured flowers, stands amid this lush
greenery, and is home to around only 2,000 inhabitants.

Parque Tropical ⋆

Continue north on the main road for a further 5 km (3 miles) until it reaches this popular birdlife centre, which has over 300 species on view, including entertaining parrot shows. ❸ At a right turning, just past the village of Guinate ❶ 928 85 55 00 ❻ Open 10.00–17.00

Mirador del Rio ⋆⋆⋆

The road reaches its most northerly point at the Mirador del Rio bar and restaurant. Arguably Lanzarote's loveliest view is from the balcony and panoramic windows of this establishment created by César Manrique at this look-out point. Inside the café, a domed white room cut into the rock looks out over a shimmering turquoise channel called El Rio to the little island of La Graciosa. ❷ 7 km (4 miles) north of Haria ❶ 928 17 35 38

Arrieta ⋆⋆

The northern road then turns sharply southward towards the south-east coast. Passing the turning to the Cueva de los Verdes (see page 87) and Jameos del Agua (see page 85), the road skirts the village of Arrieta (see page 87).

Cactus country ⋆⋆

Beyond Arrieta, the road enters Lanzarote's cactus country, an area where cactus grows freely and where it was formerly cultivated as a host plant for the cochineal beetle, which was used as the raw material for making the cochineal food dye.

Jardín de Cactus (Cactus Garden) ⋆⋆

On the approach to Guatiza an astounding 8 m (26 ft) cactus comes into view standing beside the road. It turns out to be a metal replica, made by César Manrique, and marks the entrance to his Jardín de Cactus. The garden is an amazing display of 10,000 ornamental cacti arranged in descending concentric circles. There is also a snack bar overlooking the gardens (❸ Guatiza ❶ 928 52 93 97). Continue on the same road back into Arrecife.

Timanfaya
mountains of fire

It is the hottest spot in Lanzarote. The red-streaked summit of Timanfaya rises from a solidified sea of twisted lava. Every visitor to the island is drawn to its summit. Visible from afar, the volcano dominates the view and the thoughts of visitors and locals alike. Its catastrophic force in an instant once destroyed the livelihood of most of the island, yet now it is Lanzarote's most stunning attraction. There are 36 volcanic cones within the National Park, and several others throughout the island, yet Timanfaya is the most awesome.

PARQUE NACIONAL DE TIMANFAYA

It was César Manrique who in 1970 first began the campaign to have the volcanic zone around Timanfaya made into a national park. There were already many visitors to the mountains and in that year he had opened his volcanic El Diablo restaurant. In 1974 the Parque Nacional de Timanfaya was created. Manrique designed its comical logo, a little devil with horns, tail and trident, conjuring up a sense of fiery mischief. The park extends beyond the volcanic summits to include part of the area devastated by lava and debris in the volcanic eruption of 1730.

🔻 *Parque Nacional de Timanfaya*

All access is on a single public highway that crosses one edge of the park from Yaiza to La Mancha; within the park, a turning leads off the road to a ticket booth and up to the Islote de Hilario. Cars are allowed (free parking), but the usual way to visit the site is on an inclusive bus tour from the resorts ☎ 928 84 00 57 ⏱ Open 09.00–17.00

Islote de Hilario ★★★

The car park, restaurant and start of the bus tour (see page 82) are at a location called Islote de Hilario, just below the park's highest point. This is where the lingering volcanic heat remains hottest. Ten centimetres below the surface, the temperature of the earth reaches 140°C; at 6 m (20 ft) deep it is 400°C; while just 13 m (43 ft) underground the temperature reaches 600°C. Here, wardens entertain visitors by throwing bunches of twigs into hollows where they burst into flame, and pouring buckets of cold water into holes in the ground – it roars straight back as a jet of steam. ❶ There are free parking facilities at the Islote de Hilario. The coach departs at about hourly intervals throughout the day from 10.00 to 16.00.

▶ *The volcanic landcape*

THE LATEST ERUPTIONS

The Mountains of Fire are still alive but taking a nap. The Timanfaya eruption of 1730–36 was among the longest and most powerful periods of volcanic activity ever recorded. It devastated the most agriculturally productive part of the island, turning it into a lifeless desert of ash and lava. This was followed by a series of earthquakes culminating in the eruption of the Tinguatón volcano from 1812–24. Both eruptions increased the surface area of the island, pushing the coastline out into the Atlantic. Currently there are no signs of imminent volcanic activity.

VOLCANIC LANZAROTE

All the Canary Islands were formed by volcanic eruptions millions of years ago, and some of the islands remain volcanic to this day. The island most dramatically affected by its volcanic power is Lanzarote. The southern one-third of the island contains the national park and the large area of *malpaís*, or badlands, around it, but several other parts of the island have similar landscapes, especially the Corona *malpaís* in the north-east.

THE TERRAIN

The Lanzarote *malpaís*, both inside and outside the limits of the Parque Nacional de Timanfaya, contains examples of all the kinds of volcanic material thrown forth by volcanoes: small pyroclasts (ash particles); large pyroclasts (lumps of rock shaped like a rugby ball); picón (small solid particles like pebbles); pumice (lightweight fragments of rock, often with razor-sharp edges and shot through with air bubbles); and lava (rope-like formations where liquid rock has set solid). Closer to the summits, the terrain is streaked with colour from minerals. The terrain is not entirely barren: much of it is being covered with tiny coloured lichens, while in places small plants have put down roots.

Montañas del Fuego (Mountains of Fire) bus tour ★★★

The park entrance ticket includes the fascinating 14 km (9 mile) Ruta de los Volcanes bus tour of the Montañas del Fuego (Fire Mountains), the volcanic craters of the Timafaya eruption. The bus follows a narrow, winding circular route among the peaks, giving views into volcanic cones, across collapsed underground tunnels and vistas reaching the sea. The tour takes in the **Montaña Rajada** viewpoint, the **Valle de la Tranquilidad** (Valley of Tranquility), the edge of Timanfaya itself and several smaller craters.

Camel park ★

From the foot of Timanfaya, it is possible to travel up the slope of the volcano on the back of a dromedary. Passengers travel one each side in a wooden seat, the animals being led in a line up the slope. The trip takes about 10 minutes. ⓐ 3 km (2 miles) north of Yaiza ⏱ Open 09.00–16.00

Centro de Interpretación (Mancha Blanca Interpretation Centre) ★★

The cool, peaceful Interpretation centre, most of it hidden in the ground, is one of the few man-made structures in the park. The small white building makes a startling contrast with the dark landscape. However, most of the centre lies beneath the surface, and contains exhibitions, a library, bookshop and viewpoints onto the surrounding landscape. The vibrating Eruption Hall mimics the ground movements at the time of the 1730 eruption. No smoking and no noise are allowed at the centre. ⓐ On the through-road at the northern edge of the park ⓘ 928 84 08 39 ⏱ Open 09.00–17.00

El Diablo restaurant ★★★

At the Islote del Hilario, César Manrique's restaurant and snack bar (€€) is a circle of glass walls giving superb views over the volcanic scene while visitors enjoy excellent examples of the island's specialities, especially

🔺 *Inside the Fundación César Manrique*

baked meat and bread and salty *papas arrugadas*, with local wines. The meat and fish are cooked over a large opening in the ground from which air rises from the volcano at 300°C or more. ⓐ Islote de Hilario
ⓘ 928 84 00 57 🕐 Open noon–15.30

FUNDACIÓN CÉSAR MANRIQUE

After his death in 1992, the home of Lanzarote's most influential artist César Manrique became a museum, and the headquarters of the art foundation which he had established earlier that year. However, in addition to the valuable art collection which Manrique bequeathed to Lanzarote, the house itself is one of the most fascinating sights on the island. The dazzling white walls amid the dark volcanic rock, with sharply contrasting bright flowers and well chosen cacti, the intricacy and brilliant originality of the dwelling, all together create an unforgettable experience.

The art foundation that César Manrique established was created to promote an understanding of the interaction between art, environment and culture. Its primary purpose today includes disseminating the work and intellectual legacy of César Manrique, as well as assisting the conservation and sustainable transformation of the natural environment. ⓐ Tàro de Tahiche (on road to San Bartolomé), 5 km (3 miles) north of Arrecife ⓣ 928 84 31 38 ⓕ 928 84 34 63 ⓔ fcm@fcmanrique.org ⓦ www.fcmanrique.org ⓛ Open Mon–Sat 10.00–18.00, Sun 10.00–15.00 (1 Nov–30 June); 10.00–19.00 (1 July–31 Oct)

Exterior

The visible exterior of the building, inspired by traditional local style, combines dazzling white with jet black. One of Manrique's huge wind-driven mobile artworks stands at the entrance.

Manrique had a special interest in mobiles, or wind art, and this extraordinary example is a huge, complex chaos of colour and movement. This spectacle is best seen at night, when the mobile and the house are magically dotted with light. Above the entrance, Manrique has placed his 'logo' – an interlocked C and M supposed to resemble a devil, the same image that he used for the National Park logo.

The gardens

Around the house, a lovely garden has been created between white walls and black stonework, with tiny steps and terraces. Cacti and succulents, ranging from tiny details to immense columns, are artfully arranged against the walls. It is a worthwhile to stop and relax, taking in the scents and the scenery.

Ground floor

With all-white walls, floors and ceiling, the ground floor of the house has a wonderful cool serenity, though the mood is sometimes shattered by tour guides with their groups. The whole of this floor is now a gallery of artworks from Manrique's private collection. Among them are abstract and modern works by leading 20th-century artists, including Tapies and Míro, with some line drawings by Picasso, and several of Manrique's own dramatic canvases on the theme of explosive, volcanic power.

Downstairs rooms

Beneath the beautiful but relatively conventional ground floor is Manrique's underground living area of misshapen rooms and tunnels inside bubbles in the volcanic lava. Five volcanic bubbles have been turned into rooms, each with its own colour scheme and matching specially made furniture. In one, a tree grows up through an opening in the ceiling. Openings in the rock form a narrow black and white passageway leading from one room to the next.

Outdoor terrace

Manrique used to entertain his guests in an astonishing downstairs recreational area, where an outdoor dining terrace occupies a *jameos* – a collapsed volcanic bubble open to the sky. In this enclosed space with rock walls but no ceiling are the necessities for preparing and serving a meal, including a barbecue grill, an oven and a dining table, as well as an exquisite bathing pool filled from a flowing waterspout.

On leaving the house and walking towards the exit, visitors can relax on an open terrace with a snack bar and shops located in what was formerly Manrique's garage. On sale are souvenirs, books, clothes and Manrique prints.

WHAT IS THE JAMEOS?

The volcanic areas of Lanzarote are riddled with underground tunnels formed during an eruption. A jameos is such an tunnel whose roof has collapsed, leaving it open to the sky. The Jameos del Agua is unusual in that the roof partly collapsed, but the remaining covered section concealed a clear lake.

JAMEOS DEL AGUA

An interaction of natural wonders with man's ingenuity, the Jameos del Agua (pronounced 'hameos del agwa') is one of the most remarkable sights on the island. It stands amid the dark volcanic terrain near the seashore of the Corona coast, in the north of the island. Originally an underground lake inside a volcanic tunnel in the rock, with a partly collapsed roof, the *jameos* attracted artist César Manrique. As one of his first major landscape works, he transformed the site into a delightful subterranean world of water and greenery. ⓐ Outside Arrieta
ⓘ 928 83 50 10 🕐 Jameos 11.00–18.45; nightclub Tues, Fri and Sat 19.00–15.00 (folklore show 11.00)

The underground section

From the entrance, a narrow spiral staircase descends into the ground reaching an immense cavern with still, warm air full of the sound of little birds flying around among foliage. A restaurant and nightclub dance floor stand beside a small lake. A walkway leads around the shallow transparent lake, in which resides a species of tiny blind crab that lives only here. At the far end of the lake is a bar with tables on a terrace.

The roofless section

Steps lead from the underground lake into the roofless part of the *jameos*, a cavern below sea level that is fully open to the sky. This too is a breathtaking sight. Much of the space has been turned into a clear pool with bright white and blue edging. Beyond the pool, a large cave has been fitted out as an auditorium for concerts and shows.

Casa de los Volcanes (House of Volcanoes)

More steps now climb up the side of the roofless section of the *jameos* to reach ground level again, giving views down into the beautiful open cavern. Overlooking the edge of the *jameos*, the Casa de los Volcanes (House of Volcanoes) is an all-the-family science museum mainly about volcanic activity, but with amusing push-button panels and fun displays using reflections and spatial illusions.

Corona Coast
the other malpaís

Although most of northern Lanzarote is fertile and cultivated, the barren north-east coastal area stretching almost from Arrieta to Orzola is the creation of the eruptions of the Corona volcano 5000 years ago. The Corona malpaís is riddled with curious geological rock formations.

THINGS TO SEE & DO
Arrieta ★
Lying a short distance south of the Corona *malpaís*, unspoiled Arrieta is an appealing village, with its low white houses, fishing boats and a good small beach. There are a couple of plain and simple fish restaurants at the tiny harbour. 🚌 22 km (14 miles) north of Arrecife

Cueva de los Verdes (Greens' Cave) ★★
Reached either from the Arrieta coast road or by turning off the main northern road, the Cueva de los Verdes (the name belonged to a family called Verde) is a spectacular 2 km (1 mile) section of a 7.5 km (5 mile) labyrinth of tunnels. Visitors are taken on an hour-long guided walk through an underground world with lighting and music.
📍 Near Arrieta, 1 km (0.5 mile) from Jameos del Agua ☎ 928 17 32 20
🕐 Open 10.00–18.00 (last tour 17.00) ❶ It can be slippery and the tunnel is sometimes narrow

Orzola ★
Take the coast road which skirts between the dark *malpaís* and the sea. Reaching the northern boundary of the Corona *malpaís*, and near the northern tip of Lanzarote, the road arrives at the handsome little fishing port of Orzola. There are several good, simple fish restaurants facing the water. The harbour is also used by the small ferry to the offshore Isla de la Graciosa (see page 89). 🚌 15 km (9 miles) north of Arrieta

Teguise
Lanzarote's grandest town

Founded in the 1400s, Teguise remained Lanzarote's capital for centuries and acquired several imposing buildings in grand, colonial Spanish style. They survive to this day, although Teguise is now just a small and peaceful country town, albeit with an almost African flavour. Every Sunday morning it springs to life as its narrow white cobbled streets and squares are packed with thousands of visitors for the weekly market.

HISTORY

Maciot de Bethencourt, nephew of Lanzarote's legendary Norman conqueror Jean de Bethencourt, chose to build his capital at the very centre of the island, as far as possible from the Arab raiders who constantly attacked from the sea. The site was already important as the chief meeting point of the native islanders. It remained the capital until 1852 when its port, Arrecife, overtook it in importance.

THINGS TO SEE & DO

Thanks to architecture that is almost opulent by Lanzarote standards, Teguise keeps an aristocratic air. In Plaza de la Constitución, the handsome main square, stands the town's historic principal church Iglesia de Nuestra Señora de Guadalupe. Close by, Palacio de Spinola (or Espiñola) is a grand, 18th-century private mansion now preserved as a museum. In the smaller square, Plaza 18 Julio, admire the 17th-century Casa Cuartel, originally an army barracks, and a 15th-century hospital.

Teguise Market ★★★

There is an exotic touch about the Sunday morning arts and crafts market that fills almost every one of the town's narrow lanes. Among the thousands of visitors and stallholders from the other islands there are many who have come over from west Africa, including musicians and entertainers. Local performers sometimes play folk music on traditional Canarian instruments. ◷ Open Sun 08.00–14.00

Isla de la Graciosa
a tranquil escape

The little island of La Graciosa looks its best, perhaps, when seen from the Mirador del Rio (see page 78), but for those who take the ferry across the 2 km (1 mile) wide El Rio channel for a closer look, La Graciosa is a delightful place for a day away from it all. Utterly peaceful, it consists predominantly of sand dunes with patches of volcanic terrain, with high volcanic hills in the interior, and a few green areas with vineyards and farms and windmills. For visitors, La Graciosa is a place of activities, leisure and sports, attracting sunbathers, walkers, anglers, surfers and yachtsmen.

◗ *A bird's-eye view of the Isla de la Graciosa*

The island has two tiny villages, the port of La Caleta del Sebo, an authentic fishing village where there are two simple restaurants, and La Caleta de Pedro Barba, mainly devoted to summer visitors staying in holiday homes and self-catering accommodation rentals. Both villages are located on the protected El Rio channel between the two islands. La Graciosa's total population is 500. No motor vehicles are allowed on the island, so cycling and walking are the norm. With an area of only 4144 ha (10,240 acres), the island is small enough to walk round in a day.

A day trip to La Graciosa in a modern glass-bottomed catamaran provides an easy, enjoyable way to see the island. The tour run by Líneas Marítimas Romero leaves from Orzola in the morning, with free time at La Caleta del Sebo, an excursion to the other smaller islands and the waters of the Marine Reserve, snacks and lunch on board, and a trip to a beach for swimming and exploring. Bus transfers between Orzola and the resorts are provided.

There is also a regular ferry service. Ferry crossings between La Graciosa and Orzola on Lanzarote are operated by **Líneas Marítimas Romero** ⓐ Calle García Escámez 11, Isla de La Graciosa ⓣ 928 84 20 55 ⓕ 928 84 20 69 ⓔ lmromero@lanzarote.com ⓛ The Orzola to La Graciosa ferry departs at 10.00, noon and 17.00 hours (and 18.30 hours in summer). La Graciosa to Orzola: departures at 08.00, 11.00 and 16.00 hours (and 18.00 hours in summer). The journey takes about 30 minutes each way.

THINGS TO SEE & DO
Natural park & marine reserve ★★★
In 1985, the whole island of La Graciosa was declared a natural park. Beyond La Graciosa is a cluster of tinier islands, all together forming the Chinijo Archipelago. In 1995, the whole archipelago became the Isla de la Graciosa Marine Reserve, the largest marine reserve in Europe.

An island walk ★

The ferry arrives at La Caleta del Sebo. The only road on the island, little more than a dirt track, leads away from quayside, northward towards the two volcanic hills in the centre of the island, Mojón and the twin peaks of Pedro Barba. Another small island, Montaña Clara, can be seen in the distance. Follow the track as it veers right towards La Caleta de Pedro Barba. Turn left before reaching the village to keep walking around the volcanic Pedro Barba peaks, keeping the mountain on your left. Another peak, Montaña Bermeja, rises on the right. Straight ahead is a beautiful coastline of dark rocky outcrops and a long sandy beach, Playa de las Conchas. The island of Alegranza can be seen in the distance.

Before the beach, turn left at an intersection of paths, to take a southward direction back towards La Caleta del Sebo. The Mojón volcano is now on the right, the two Pedro Barba crests on the left. There is a good view of the sheer Famara cliffs ahead. The path returns into La Caleta del Sebo. The walk takes around four hours. Do remember to wear a hat and take enough water and food because there is no shade along the route.

⬇ *Examining the day's catch*

EXCURSIONS

Fuerteventura & Lobos
island neighbours

A day trip to Fuerteventura is a major attraction. Lanzarote's much larger neighbour is just 40 minutes away on a pleasant sea crossing. For anyone staying in the resort of Playa Blanca, where the regular ferry leaves from, it is too convenient to resist. For others, frequent inclusive excursions are organized by tour operators and local travel agencies. Many inclusive trips also take in a visit to tiny Lobos Island, just off the north coast of Fuerteventura.

FUERTEVENTURA

Closest to Africa, the island of Fuerteventura feels like an offshoot of the Sahara, hot, dry, empty and sandy. The name means 'strong winds', and although these blow only occasionally, they are strong enough to have brought enough sand to create immense dunes on the east coast. The island is the least populous of all the larger Canaries, and over half the inhabitants live in the small capital town, Puerto del Rosario. The poet Unamuno described Fuerteventura as 'an oasis in the desert that is civilization'.

Ferries run by the Fred Olsen Line (❸ 928 53 50 90) travel between Playa Blanca and Corralejo several times daily. The trip across the 11 km (7 mile) channel between the two islands takes 40 minutes. Alternatively take a full-day inclusive excursion on, for example, the *Cesar II*, which includes bathing platforms and a lunch on board, allows 2 hours on shore at Corralejo, and also takes in a trip to the island of Lobos.
ⓐ *Cesar II* office at the harbour ❸ 928 81 36 08 ❹ Excursions Mon–Fri
❶ €43 per adult, children €23

Corralejo Town ★★★

A busy working harbour and a pleasant, small town with plenty of bars and restaurants, and with some nightlife, this is northern Fuerteventura's main resort. There is a small beach of white sand close to the town centre, but more interesting are the vast golden beaches on

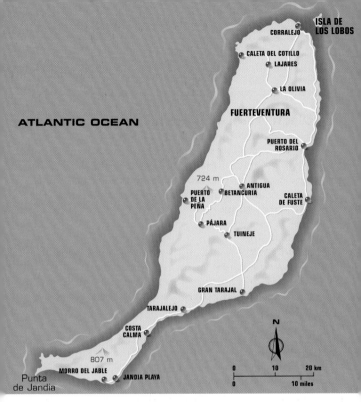

the southern edge of town and beyond. There is a tourist office in Plaza Grande (☎ 928 86 62 35)

Sand dunes ★★★

It is worth taking a trip on foot or by taxi to see the extraordinary dunes of pale sand that extend for 10 km (6 miles) along the seashore south from Corralejo, and reach about 3 km (2 miles) inland. This desert zone has the protected status of a national park, the Parque National de las Dunas de Corralejo. For the tourist, the main attraction may be beautiful beaches, but for the scientist the sands are of interest for some unusual plant varieties that can live in such an environment, including the

yellow-flowering lotus shrub and the bluebell-like echium. Some limited development has been permitted on the park's beachfront.

ISLA DE LOS LOBOS (ISLAND OF SEALS)

This unspoiled, unihabited little island 3 km (2 miles) from Corralejo makes an enjoyable addition to a trip to Fuerteventura. It probably takes its name, 'Island of Seals', from the curious, seal-like shapes of dark volcanic rock emerging from the pale sands of the shore. Although many visitors pause here to swim, sunbathe or walk, it remains wonderfully tranquil. Remember to bring a hat, drinking water and something to eat, as there are no facilities on the island.

RESTAURANTS

La Marquesina €€ Close to the harbour jetty, waterside tables provide an enjoyable view of boats coming and going as you enjoy the fresh fish specialities. ⓐ Calle El Muelle Chico, Fuerteventura ❶ 928 53 54 35 ⓛ Open all day

Rosie O'Grady's € Live music nightly, tasty home-cooked familiar dishes from home and a lively atmosphere make this Irish pub one of the most popular spots in town. ⓐ Calle Pizarro 10, Corralejo, Fuerteventura ❶ 928 86 75 63 ⓛ Open from 19.00

Sotavento €€ A big menu of well-prepared fish and seafood makes this one of the best places to eat in Corralejo. There is a choice of meat dishes, too, with a few snacks and an inexpensive children's menu as well. ⓐ Avenida Maritima 7, Corralejo, Fuerteventura ❶ 928 53 64 17 ⓛ Open all day

LIFESTYLE
Island life

LIFESTYLE

Food & drink
eating out

Canarios, like other Spaniards, love to eat out with friends and family, tucking into their food with a robust appetite, sharing noisy, convivial conversation, and letting children run and play around the table (there is no Spanish word for 'bedtime', and parents rarely go out without their children). Only the very smartest places demand any degree of formality. Apart from a light early breakfast of coffee and a pastry, meal times tend to be late by north European standards; about 14.00 for lunch and 21.00 for dinner. However, an exception is made for tourists. In the resorts, meals are served at all times of day. It is not unusual to see locals finishing lunch while tourists are beginning their evening meal. Hotel dining rooms often serve dinner at 19.00 hours.

INTERNATIONAL EATING

It would be perfectly possible to spend a fortnight on the island and have nothing but Italian food, for example – and many holidaymakers do just that. With the local population so outnumbered by tourists, restaurants increasingly offer an international dining experience, with a variety of familiar home-from-home dishes like soups, steak and chips or omelettes. Chinese, Thai, Indian and most other ethnic styles are also widely available. Popular Spanish dishes like paella, not part of the Canaries cuisine, make an appearance too.

LOCAL FOOD

Most visitors to Lanzarote eat little, if any, of the local cooking. Yet Lanzarote has a repertoire of its own of delicious local dishes. These are generally available in the more authentic bars or restaurants. When touring the island, look for restaurants called *tipico*, meaning 'local style'. The local cuisine is a blend of three main influences. Most of all, it is Canarian, all the islands sharing a common culinary heritage, but Lanzarote has some of its own individual elements, such as a special fondness for meat stews. Least of all, it is Spanish, but it does share a few elements with the food of the mainland, such as the tradition of tapas – substantial appetizers that can make a meal in themselves.

FISH

Since most of the coastal resorts were formerly fishing ports, it is not surprising that fish is an island staple. More unexpected is that on Lanzarote traditionally fish is salted and preserved instead of being eaten fresh. Among the most popular local specialities is *Pescado a la sal*, fish baked in salt; another is *Sancocho*, a thick stew of salted fish and vegetables. Freshly caught fish was traditionally eaten only on the coast, but is now widely available. The most common fish on the menu, *abade*, *cabrilla*, *cherne* and *mero*, are all varieties of sea bass. *Vieja*, parrot fish, and *merluza*, hake, also make a frequent appearance. Fresh fish is usually prepared very simply, grilled or fried, and often served with a spicy *mojo* sauce. Another local dish is *espada*, swordfish. There is plenty of seafood too, such as *calamares* (deep fried rings of squid), *pulpo* (octopus) and shellfish, especially *gambas* (prawns).

MEAT

Wild game and pork are the favourite foods of Lanzaroteños. Rabbit, *conejo*, is especially well liked and inexpensive, and often appears on menus. *Conejo con salmorejo*, rabbit cooked in a spicy tomato sauce, is a Canarian classic. Another mouth-watering island speciality is roast leg of pork. The most popular way to cook meat is in a hearty, rich, savoury stew with plenty of meat cooked with vegetables and pulses like chickpeas, lentils or beans. Today, this is the dish par excellence, to eat at leisure with friends and family. Meat stews frequently combine several meats in the same pot, typically rabbit and pork. For a touch of tradition, the soup may be thickened with *gofio*.

MEAT STEWS

Puchero is a classic Lanzarote stew, thick and savoury, made with lentils, chickpeas, vegetables and two or more kinds of meat, including pork. Similar is *rancho canario*, though with more vegetables and less meat.

Vegetarians beware – even *potaje*, or vegetable stew, or stews with names like *potaje de berros* (watercress soup), contain meat. For locals, such a dish served with bread and wine makes a complete meal, but in restaurants a small portion may be offered as a starter.

MOJO

The most uniquely Canarian phrase on the menu is *con mojo*, 'with *mojo*'. Grilled or fried fish, roasted meats, or boiled vegetables, almost anything may be served *con mojo*. *Mojo* (pronounced 'mo-ho') is the piquant sauce of the Canary Islands. Based on olive oil, it comes in different versions, and in good restaurants is more or less spicy according to what it accompanies. *Mojo* comes in two colours – red and green. Coriander and parsley make *mojo verde*, green *mojo*, which has a refreshing bite, while hot chillis are are used in the spicier *mojo rojo*, red *mojo*.

CHEESES

Mojo is the perfect accompaniment for fried or grilled goat's cheese, served as a delicious starter. Cheese has an important part in the local diet, and is often eaten as tapas or with a glass of wine. Although Lanzarote does produce goat's cheeses called *conejero*, the best and most important cheese is brought over from neighbouring Fuerteventura. Called *majorero*, this traditional Fuerteventura speciality is a gourmet's delight, acclaimed throughout Spain. *Majorero* is a mix of goat's and sheep's milk with a dense texture and strong but smooth flavour. Older *majorero* can be coated with oil and paprika or *gofio*.

VEGETABLES

Lanzarote does not have abundant fruit and vegetables. The exceptions are *batatas* (sweet potatoes), *cebollas* (onions), and above all, *papas* (potatoes). The potatoes are almost invariable eaten as the famous Canarian speciality, *papas arrugadas*, literally 'wrinkly potatoes'. These are new potatoes boiled in their skins in very salty water, leaving them with a crunchy coating of salt. Usually served *con mojo*, they are delicious with meat, fish or cheese, or on their own.

GOFIO

It was the *Guanches*, the native Canary islanders wiped out by the Spanish, who invented this rough roasted wholemeal flour. Used as a thickener in stews, or mixed into vegetable dishes, it can also be eaten on its own like a grain for savoury dishes or as a flour baked into sweet puddings.

DESSERTS

Canarios have a sweet tooth, and may finish a meal with the islanders' traditional dessert, *bienmesabe*, a heavy, syrupy, nutty concoction. It is often served with ice cream. As an alternative, try the chocolate version. *Gofio* desserts are rather stodgy and syrupy, but if you would like to try one, sample *flan gofio* or *frangollo*.

WINES

Many Canarios are likely to order a Spanish beer with their food, but the discerning may choose one of the island's local wines. Unlike other Canary Islands, Lanzarote produces excellent fine wines, crisp, dry and white, made from the malvasia grape. Curiously, the very best come from the least likely terrain, the inhospitable *malpaís* of the La Geria Valley, where the grape bushes have to be protected from sun and wind in order to survive. One of the La Geria *bodegas*, or wineries, is the oldest in the Canary Islands: Bodegas El Grifo, founded in 1775, is considered one of the leading wineries (☎ 928 52 40 36 ⓦ www.elgrifo.com). Finish off with a tot of *ronmiel*, rum-honey. This is made from something truly unique to the Canaries, palm tree sap, gathered on the island of La Gomera.

● *The excellent local wine*

Menu decoder

aceitunas en mojo Olives in hot sauce
bocadillo (bocadee-yo) Filled roll
ensalada Salad

helado Ice cream
perrito caliente Hot-dog
tapas Snacks

TYPICAL CANARIAN DISHES

cabrito Kid (goat)

caldo de escado Fish, vegetables and maize meal stew

chipirones Small squid

conejo al salmorejo Rabbit in hot chilli sauce

gambas ajillo Garlic prawns

garbanzasa Chickpea stew with meat

lomo Slices of pork

pata de cerdo Roast leg of pork

pechuga empanada Breaded chicken breast or chicken breast
   in batter

potage Thick vegetable soup – may contain added meat

potage de berros Watercress soup

puchero Meat and vegetable stew

queso Cheese

ranchos Noodles, beef and chickpeas

ropa vieja Chickpeas, vegetables and potatoes (although meat can be
   added)

sancocho Salted fish (often *cherne*, a kind of sea bass) with potatoes
   and sweet potatoes

DESSERTS

arroz con leche Cold rice pudding

bienmesabe A mix of honey and almonds (delicious poured over
   ice cream)

flan Crème caramel

fruta del tiempo Fresh fruit in season

truchas Turnovers filled with pumpkin jam

Papas arrugadas (small jacket potatoes boiled in very salty water) served with a *mojo picante* (hot chilli sauce) or *mojo verde* (herb and garlic sauce) make an ideal snack at lunchtime. Those with a light appetite might find one dish between two is sufficient.

DRINKS

agua (pronounced *ah-whah*)

mineral Mineral water
con gas/sin gas Fizzy/still

batido Milkshake
café Coffee

con leche Made with milk
cortado Small white coffee
descafeinado Decaffeinated
solo Black

cerveza Beer
leche Milk
limonada Lemonade
naranja Orange
ron Local rum
té Tea
vino Wine

blanco White
rosado Rosé
tinto Red

SPECIALITY DRINKS

bitter kas Similar to Campari but non-alcoholic
Cocktail Atlantico Rum, dry gin, banana liqueur, blue curaçao, pineapple nectar
Cocktail Canario Rum, banana cream liqueur, orange juice, cointreau, a drop of grenadine
guindilla Rum-based cherry liqueur
mora Blackberry liqueur
ron miel Rum-with honey, a local speciality
sangria Mix of red wine, spirits and fruit juices; can be made with champagne on request

Shopping

TEGUISE

A tourist attraction as much as a market, the weekly Sunday morning market fills all the town-centre streets of this handsome old town. Many thousands arrive to mingle, relax, stroll, eat and drink, enjoy the buskers and maybe buy something. The goods for sale are souvenirs, toys and hippie-style crafts (few traders are locals). Worth looking for, though, are stallholders with displays of good Spanish lace and embroidery.

ARRECIFE

Every weekday morning from 06.30 hours to noon Lanzarote's busy capital has fish and produce markets in **Calle Liebre**, where the house-wives of the town choose the best ingredients for the family dinner. If you are self-catering, join them. At the fish market, look for the sign '*Pescado del Barquillo*' – literally little-boat fish – for the freshest catch which has just been brought in by the fishermen.

COSTA TEGUISE

Every Friday night from around 18.00 hours, Costa Teguise has its after-dark street market in and around the pedestrianized **Plaza Pueblo Marinero**, where traders sell their own handmade craft work in a relaxed atmosphere.

SMALLER MARKETS

The resort of **Playa Blanca** and the northern country town of **Haría** both have markets every Saturday morning (approx. 10.00–14.00 hours). These are relaxed, colourful events where some stallholders sell a little food and fresh produce, but the emphasis is on handmade arts and crafts, souvenirs, linens, clothes and other fabrics, ceramics and knick-knacks.

LACE & EMBROIDERY

Available in better-quality shops are attractive, elegant fabrics, lacework and embroideries with distinctively Spanish designs, such as tablecloths and napkins, sheets and pillowcases, and handkerchiefs. These are not cheap, but represent excellent value for skilful workmanship.

CERAMICS

Traditional Spanish glazed pottery, including crockery as well as tiles and other ceramics, are distinctive and attractive. With the airlines' luggage allowance in mind, look out for smaller items.

'TAX-FREE' GOODS

The Canaries are no longer a duty-free region but they still benefit from lower taxes. Numerous shops called 'bazars' claim to be selling 'tax-free' goods. They stock a huge array of imported items.

MANRIQUE MERCHANDISE

Stylish, well-made T-shirts and other clothes printed with eyecatching Manrique designs or his CM personal logo are at the **Fundacíon César Manrique** shop (❸ Taro de Tahiche ☎ 928 81 01 38), or at resort branches.

OUT OF AFRICA

Vividly dressed African traders can simply catch a boat from Senegal to the Canaries, bringing all manner of exotic merchandise. You will find them at the markets and resorts, selling African drums, wooden masks, toys and elaborately tooled leatherwork. Do not buy smuggled historic ceremonial items and ivory goods (illegal in the EU).

SEMI-PRECIOUS STONES

Polished semi-precious stones make unusual, attractive souvenirs or gifts. Look out for the locally gathered green stone here called *olivina*, also known as chrysolite, evening emerald or peridot.

Beware – prices are often no lower than in the UK. But shoppers who have done their research can pick up a bargain. Try RT Electronics, at Centro Comercial Jameos Playa, Playa de los Pocillos.

Kids

For children like for grown-ups, the whole island is full of interest and entertainment. The easy-going, tolerant attitude to children, both in the resorts and in the inland villages, ensures that they too have a good holiday. They are almost always welcomed, whether into restaurants, bars or entertainments.

Some of the main sights are rewarding for all the family. Children will be as awed as their parents by the water and fire display on Timanfaya (see page 79). The Fundación César Manrique (see page 77), too, will astonish them – when they see that Manrique lived in five air bubbles under the ground. And the whirring, colourful mobiles that Manrique erected at several road junctions on the island are like giant baby toys.

TOP ACTIVITIES
Submarine Safaris ★★★
Dive into the deeps on the Yellow Submarine *Sub Fun III* and see a different world through the large viewports. It is air conditioned, with air pressure maintained at normal atmospheric levels. No children under two years of age permitted. ⓐ Submarine Safaris SL, Puerto Calero marina ⓣ 928 51 28 98 or 928 51 29 06 ⓔ info@submarinesafaris.com ⓦ www.submarinesafaris.com ⓛ Excursions at 10.00, noon, 14.00 and 16.00

Aqua Park ★★
Colourful water slides and flumes, gentle rides for the youngest toddlers, a bouncy castle and more thrilling options for teenagers. ⓐ Avda Club De Golf ⓣ 928 59 21 28 ⓛ Open 10.00–18.00

Boat excursions ★★
For most children, just to have a trip in a boat is a thrill. The child-oriented Pirate Cruise is one of the many options on offer at Playa Blanca. Ask representatives for details.

Go-karting ★★

On the main highway near Puerto del Carmen **Gran Karting Club Lanzarote** has something for (nearly) all ages. There is a junior track for ages 12–16, mini-karts for the over fives, while children over ten can also try their hand on mini motorcycles called mini-bikes. ⓐ La Rinconada, National Highway ❶ 619 75 99 46 Ⓦ www.vista-lanzarote.com
🕓 10.00–22.00 (summer); 10.00–21.00 (winter)

Horse riding ★★

The excellent equestrian activities centre **Lanzarote a Caballo**, about 4 km (2.5 miles) from Puerto Calero, offers riding tours and activities for all ages and all levels, including guided sightseeing tours, and a children's section called Fort Apache. ⓐ Carretera Arrecife-Yaiza, Km 17 ❶ 928 83 03 14 ⓔ lanzaroteacaballo@lanzarote.com

Rancho Texas Lanzarote ★★

This activity and entertainment centre on a Wild West theme has plenty to interest children, including shows with birds of prey and alligators several times daily. ⓐ Calle Noruega, 35510 Tías ❶ 928 84 12 86
ⓔ ranchotexas@lanzarote.com Ⓦ www.ranchotexaslanzarote.com

Canarian Cetacean Museum ★

This fascinating museum is all about the whale and dolphin family. Visitors find out about the Canary Islands' ocean enviroment and learn about these remarkable creatures through images, sound, full-size replicas and biological exhibits. ❶ 928 84 95 60 ❶ 928 84 95 61
ⓔ info@museodecetaceos.org Ⓦ www.museodecetaceos.org
🕓 Open 11.00–19.00 (summer); 10.00–18.00 (winter).

Guinate Parque Tropical (Guinate Tropical Park) ★

Way up in the north of the island, give the children a break at this popular, child-friendly birdlife centre, which has over 300 species on view, including entertaining parrot shows. ⓐ Guinate ❶ 928 85 55 00
🕓 Open 10.00–17.00

Festivals & events

Lanzaroteños love a fiesta as much as anyone in Spain. All the festivals and events that they celebrate with such energy are at heart religious, though with a strong element of music, food and having fun.

CARNIVAL

The highlight of Lanzarote's year is the frenzied celebration of Carnival in February, focused mainly near the waterfronts of Arrecife and Puerto del Carmen. It brings at least a week of street parties, a fantastic costume parade accompanied by whistles and drums. On Ash Wednesday there's a bizarre climax, the 'Entierro de la Sardinas', or Burial of the Sardine.

Future carnivals: 28 Feb 2006; 20 Feb 2007; 5 Feb 2008

● *Join in the lively local festivals*

CORPUS CHRISTI

Taking place in June (sometimes late May), this is a dignified, fascinating Catholic festival enthusiastically celebrated in Lanzarote. While in other parts of Spain, the streets are carpeted with flowers, in Lanzarote's version pavements and squares in Arrecife are decorated with *Alfombras del Sal*, elaborate pictures in brightly coloured dyed sea salt.

FIESTA DE SAN JUAN

Three days of bonfires, parties and traditional events celebrate the summer solstice, from 21 to 24 June, culminating in St John's Day or Midsummer's Day, on the 24th. The centre of celebration is the town of Haría and its 'Valley of 1000 Palm Trees' in the north of the island.

FIESTA DEL VIRGEN DEL CARMEN

The fishing ports and coastal towns pay homage to Our Lady the Virgin of Carmen on 16 July. The main focus is Puerto del Carmen, where a decorated statue of the Virgin heads a big procession through the streets before being taken onto fishing boats in the harbour.

FIESTA DE SAN GINÈS

The islanders say San Ginés watches over their seafaring tradition and protects their sailors and fishermen. In August, the saint is honoured in grand style in all the island's towns with many days of processions, parades and folk dancing in the streets. The centre of activity is Arrecife's Church of San Ginés, beside El Charco lagoon in the town centre.

VIRGEN DE LOS VOLCANES

During the volcanic eruption of 1824, the residents of Mancha Blanca and Tinguaton prayed to the Virgin to stop the lava reaching their village. Their prayers were heard and the lava came to a halt at the edge of the village. Today islanders flock to the Hermitage of the Sorrows outside Mancha Blanca on 15 september, where volcanic *malpaís* meets green farmland, to honour the Virgin of the Volcanoes.

CALENDAR OF FIESTAS

5 January	Cabalgata de los Reyes Magos Festival, Teguise
February	Carnival
March/April	Village events all over the island at Easter
15 May	Fiesta de San Isidro, Uga
24 June	Fiesta de San Juan
June	Corpus Christi
7 July	Fiesta de San Marcial del Rubicón, Femés
16 July	Fiesta de Nuestra Señora del Carmen
25 August	Fiesta de San Ginés
8 September	Fiesta de Nuestra Señora de Guadalupe, Teguise
	Fiesta de Nuestra Señora de los Remedios, Yaiza
15 September	Virgen de los Volcanes

Sports & activities

Lanzarote has a well-deserved reputation as a sports island, an ideal place for activities on both land and water. Walking, riding and cycling are readily available. Puerto Calero on the south coast is the sailing resort par excellence, while Famara on the north coast is renowned among windsurfers and paragliders. Lanzarote also has one of the world's leading sports and activities resorts, Club La Santa, on the north coast.

LA SANTA SPORTS

Club La Santa, at La Santa Sport 12 km (7 miles) west of La Caleta de Famara, is the world's premier residential sports resort, with first-class equipment and facilities including an Olympic pool. It is the setting for major international sports and athletics events, including the tough Ironman Triathlon. Day visitors are welcome to the resort, but residential stays must be booked well in advance, through your local agent.
UK agents: Sports Tours Int. ⓐ 91 Walkden Rd, Walkden, Worsley M28 5DQ Manchester, UK ⓣ 0161 790 9890 ⓕ 0161 790 9811 ⓔ info@clublasanta.co.uk ⓦ www.clublasanta.co.uk

CYCLING

Bikes can be hired at all the resorts. As well as easy beachside riding, there are more challenging routes in the interior of the island. Companies like **MegaFun** have a wide variety of bikes and other machines. ⓐ Playa de los Pocillos ⓣ 928 51 28 93 ⓦ www.megafun-lanzarote.com

DIVING

Costa Teguise, Puerto Calero and Playa Blanca have several diving centres. The two top names in Lanzarote diving and scuba are: the long-established **Calipso Diving** ⓐ Centro Comercial Nautical, Avenida de los Islas Canarias, Costa Teguise ⓣ 928 59 08 79 ⓔ Calipso@arrakis.es ⓦ www.calipso-diving.com ⓛ Mon–Sat 09.00–18.00, closed Sun; and

The Dive Centre ⓐ Puerto Calero Marina ⓣ 928 51 18 80
ⓔ info@divelanzarote.com ⓦ www.divelanzarote.com

GO-KARTING

Close to Matagorda, on the main highway just past the Puerto del
Carmen turn-off, is **Gran Karting Club Lanzarote**, an excellent track for
all ages. The senior track allows speeds up to 80 km/h (50 mph), while
the junior track (ages 12–16) gives a chance to try driving at safer speeds.
There are mini-karts for the over fives; children over 10 can also try mini
motorcycles. ⓐ La Rinconada, National Highway ⓣ 619 75 99 46
ⓦ www.vista- lanzarote.com ⓛ 10.00–22.00 (summer); 10.00–21.00 (winter)

GOLF

The attractive 18-hole **Costa Teguise Golf Club** is considered to be one of
the great places in the world to play golf. The club is open to visitors at
all levels and lessons and equipment hire are also available. ⓐ Avda del
Golf, Costa Teguise ⓣ 928 59 05 12 ⓔ lanzarotegolf@lanzarote.com
ⓦ www.lanzarote-golf.com

RIDING
Lanzarote a Caballo

Lanzarote a Caballo is an equestrian activity centre offering horse riding
for all levels at the site, to explore the local countryside on horseback, or
to go on guided sightseeing tours of the island. ⓐ Carretera Arrecife-
Yaiza, Km 17 (on the main highway between the Puerto Calero and Playa
Quemada junctions) ⓣ 928 83 03 14 or 626 64 73 68 ⓕ 928 81 39 95
ⓔ lanzaroteacaballo@lanzarote.com ⓦ www.lanzaroteacaballo.com

Rancho Texas Lanzarote

Rancho Texas is an activity and leisure centre based on horse riding, but
also with other entertainment, including children's attractions. Among
the horse-riding options are a three-hour trek for experienced riders and
a one-hour trek for beginners. ⓐ Calle Noruega, 35510 Tías ⓣ 928 84 12 86
ⓦ www.ranchotexaslanzarote.com

SURFING

Surfing facilities are available at all the resorts. Famara (see page 31), on the north coast, is a leading European surfing resort. Among the surfing outfits based there are long-established Surf School Lanzarote and Calimasurf, who organize residential surfing camps.

Calimasurf ⓐ Calle Achique 14 ① 626 91 33 69 (open 10.00–21.00) ⓔ info@calimasurf.com ⓦ www.calimasurf.com

Surf School Lanzarote ⓐ La Caleta de Famara ① 928 52 86 23 or mobile 686 00 49 09 (09.00–10.00 and 17.00–18.00) ⓦ www.surfschoollanzarote.com

WALKING

Timanfaya Walks

Properly equipped walkers can join guided tours on two marked paths within the Parque Nacional de Timanfaya. The 3 km (2 mile) **Tremesana Trail** takes around two hours, exploring the *malpaís* area close to the camel park north of Yaiza. The commentary (Spanish and English) explains the detail of the volcanic terrain and the reappearing vegetation. The tougher 9 km (6 mile) **Ruta del Litoral** takes about five hours, exploring the undeveloped, unvisited volcanic coast on the western edge of the park. To enquire or book, contact the Mancha Blanca Interpretation Centre, on the through-road at the northern edge of the Park. ① 928 84 08 39 ⓒ Open 09.00–17.00

Canary Trekking

Lanzarote's network of footpaths is opened up by **Canary Trekking**, based at Costa Teguise, who put together guided walks in all parts of the island. ⓐ Calle La Laguna 18, casa 1, Costa Teguise ① 609.53 76 84

WINDSURFING

Windsurfing is available at all the resorts, and is especially recommended at Costa Teguise and Playa de los Pocillos. Windsurf Paradise ⓐ Calle La Corvina 8, Costa Teguise ① 928 34 60 22

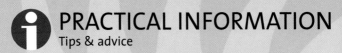

PRACTICAL INFORMATION
Tips & advice

Preparing to go

GETTING THERE

By far the easiest and least expensive way to visit Lanzarote is on a package holiday. Inclusive packages, operated by all the major travel companies, leave from all over northern Europe several times weekly. You will find tour operators featuring Lanzarote at: Ⓦ www.abta.com

For travellers who already have accommodation in Lanzarote, or wish to book hotels directly, both charter and scheduled airlines sell low-cost direct flights to the island from London and most UK regional airports. Find low-cost flights on: Ⓦ www.cheapflights.co.uk. You should also check the travel supplements of the weekend newspapers, such as the *Sunday Telegraph* and the *Sunday Times*. They often carry adverts for inexpensive flights. For more visitor information contact the **Spanish Tourist Office** Ⓐ UK office: PO Box 4009, London W1A 6NB
Ⓣ 020 7486 8077 Ⓕ 020 7486 8034 Ⓔ tourspain@latestinfo.co.uk
Ⓦ www.spain.info Ⓛ Open 09.15–16.15, Mon–Fri Ⓐ Republic of Ireland office: PO Box 10015, Dublin 1 Ⓛ Open 09.15–16.15, Mon–Fri
24-hour brochure request line Ⓣ UK:08459 400 180 Ⓣ Republic of Ireland: 0818 220 290 ❶ Calls are charged at national rates

BEFORE YOU LEAVE

All EU and US citizens are free to travel to Lanzarote. No inoculations or health preparations are needed. It is a good idea to pack a small first-aid kit to carry with you containing plasters, antiseptic cream, travel-sickness pills, insect repellent and/or bite-relief cream, antihistamine tablets, upset stomach remedies and painkillers. Sun lotion can be more expensive in Lanzarote than in the UK, so it is worth taking a good selection, especially of the higher factor lotions if you have children with you, and do not forget after-sun cream as well. If you are taking prescription medicines, ensure that you take enough for the duration of your visit, and an extra copy of the information sheet in case of loss, but you may find it impossible to obtain the same medicines in Lanzarote. It is also worth having a dental check-up before you leave the UK.

DOCUMENTS

The most important documents you will need are your tickets and your passport. Check well in advance that your passport is up to date and has at least three months left to run (6 months is even better). All children, including newborn babies, need their own passport now. It generally takes at least 3 weeks to process a passport renewal. This can be longer in the run-up to the summer months. Contact the **Passport Agency** for the latest information on how to renew your passport and the processing times involved. ☎ 0870 521 0410 Ⓦ www.ukpa.gov.uk.

You should check the details of your travel tickets well before your departure, ensuring that the timings and dates are correct.

If you are thinking of hiring a car while you are away, you will need to have your UK driving licence with you. If you want more than one driver for the car, the other drivers must have their licences too.

MONEY

You will need some currency before you go, especially if your flight gets you to your destination at the weekend or late in the day after the banks have closed. Travellers' cheques are the safest way to carry money because the money will be refunded if the cheques are lost or stolen. To buy travellers' cheques or exchange money at a bank you may need to give up to a week's notice, depending on the quantity of foreign currency you require. You can exchange money at the airport before you depart. You should also make sure that your credit, charge and debit cards are up to date – you do not want them to expire mid-holiday – and that your credit limit is sufficient to allow you to make those holiday purchases. Once you arrive, you will find cash dispensers in all the resorts. Do not forget, too, to check your PIN numbers in case you have not used them for a while – you may want to draw money while you are away. Ring your bank or card company and they will help you out.

INSURANCE

Do you have sufficient cover for your holiday? Check that your policy covers you adequately for loss of possessions and valuables, for activities you might want to try – such as scuba diving, horse riding, or water sports – and for emergency medical and dental treatment, including flights home if required.

It is essential to take an E111 form (available from post offices) to take with you, to ensure that if you have any medical treatment while away you can reclaim the costs incurred on your return. After January 2006, a new EHIC card replaces the E111 form to allow UK-visitors access to reduced-cost and sometimes free state-provided medical treatment in the EEA. For further information, ring EHIC enquiries line: ☎ 0845 605 0707 or visit the Department of Health website: 🌐 www.dh.gov.uk

CLIMATE

Daytime temperatures do not vary greatly throughout the year, although there is light rain sometimes, Almost all the rain falls in the winter, but even in the wettest months (Dec/Jan) rainfall totals average only 2.7 cm (just over 1 in) per month. However, it can be chilly in the evenings during the winter months, so it is advisable to take something warmer for the evenings, a shawl or jacket.

Be sure that young children wear something on their heads, because the UV rays are strong and when there is a breeze the sun can feel deceptively cooler than it actually is.

SECURITY

Take sensible precautions to while you are away:

- Cancel milk, newspapers and other regular deliveries so that post and milk do not pile up on the doorstep.
- Let the postman know where to leave bulky mail (ideally with a next-door neighbour) that will not go through your letterbox.

TELEPHONING LANZAROTE

To call Lanzarote from the UK, dial 00 34 then the nine-digit number – there's no need to wait for a dialling tone.

- If possible, arrange for a friend or neighbour to visit regularly, closing and opening your curtains, and switching the lights on and off. Or consider buying electrical timing devices that will switch lights and radios on and off
- Let Neighbourhood Watch representatives know that you will be away so that they can keep an eye on your home.
- If you have a burglar alarm, make sure that it is working properly and is switched on when you leave (you may find that your insurance policy requires this). Ensure that a neighbour is able to gain access to the alarm to turn it off, just in case it is set off accidentally.
- If you are leaving cars unattended, put them in a garage, if possible, and leave a key with a neighbour in case the alarm goes off.

AIRPORT PARKING & ACCOMMODATION

If you intend to leave your car in an airport car park while you are away, or stay the night at an airport hotel before or after your flight, you should book well ahead to take advantage of discounts or cheap off-airport parking. Airport accommodation gets booked up several weeks in advance, especially during the height of the holiday season. Check whether the hotel offers free parking for the duration of the holiday – often the savings made on parking costs can significantly reduce the accommodation price.

BAGGAGE ALLOWANCE

Baggage allowances vary according to the airline, destination and class of travel, but 20 kg (44 lb) per person is the norm for luggage that is carried in the hold (it usually tells you what the weight limit is on your ticket). You are also allowed one item of cabin baggage weighing no more than 5 kg (11 lb), and measuring 46 by 30 by 23 cm (18 by 12 by 9 in). In addition, you can usually carry your duty-free purchases, umbrella, handbag, coat, camera, etc. as hand baggage. Large items – surfboards, golf-clubs, collapsible wheelchairs and pushchairs – are usually charged as extras and it is a good idea to let the airline know in advance if you want to bring these.

CHECK-IN, PASSPORT CONTROL & CUSTOMS

First-time travellers can often find airport security intimidating, but it is all very easy, really.

- Check-in desks usually open two or three hours before the flight is due to depart. Arrive early for the best choice of seats.
- Look for your flight number on the TV monitors in the check-in area, and find the relevant check-in desk. Your tickets will be checked and your luggage taken. Take your boarding card and go to the departure gate. Here your hand luggage will be X-rayed and your passport checked.
- In the departure area, you can shop and relax, but watch the monitors that tell you when to board – usually about 30 minutes before take-off. Go to the departure gate shown on the monitor and follow the instructions given to you by the airline staff.

During your stay

BEACHES

In summer, many beaches have lifeguards and a flag safety system. There are some safe and beautiful beaches on the islands, some golden sand and a few black sand, and there are many blue flag beaches, which denote that they are clean and safe.

The sea, however, does not respect blue flags, and care must always be taken to observe changes in the wind, which may whip up a rough sea, or change the tide direction. Always observe the red flags; do not think that you are a strong swimmer and nothing could happen to you

BEACH SAFETY

A flag system is used to warn bathers when sea conditions are unsafe for swimming.

- Red flag: dangerous conditions, no swimming
- Yellow: good swimmers only, apply caution
- Green: safe bathing conditions

because where these flags fly the currents are dangerous, with undertows. Other beaches may be safe for swimming but there are unlikely to be lifeguards or life-saving amenities available. If in doubt, ask your local representative or hotel.

You will notice that the beaches are free of litter; it is up to everyone to keep them so. In fact, one of the lovely things about Lanzarote is the cleanliness of the villages – the people take a pride in looking after them.

CHILDREN'S ACTIVITIES

Most islanders love children – in a busy Canarian bar, if a child struggles up onto a stool and asks for a glass of water, they will be served immediately. You will find that nearly all villages have designated playground areas, with an abundance of swings, slides and other amusements, all free. Children are welcome everywhere, and the islands are at present safe from child-related crime, so you can relax and enjoy all that there is on offer.

CONSULATE

The **British Consulate Las Palmas** on the island of Gran Canaria is the nearest British consul. ⓐ Consular Section, Calle Luis Morte 9 – 3rd floor, Las Palmas de Gran Canaria, Canary Islands ⓣ 928 26 25 08/26 58 ⓕ 928 26 77 74 ⓔ Laspalmasconsulate@ukinspain.com

CURRENCY

Lanzarote, as part of Spain, is in the euro zone, throughout which the currency is the Euro (€). One Euro is divided into 100 euro cents. Euro note denominations are 500, 200, 100, 50, 20, 10 and 5. Coins are 1 and 2 Euros and 1, 2, 5, 10, 20 and 50 céntimos. Cash and credit cards are the main methods of payment – cheques are rarely accepted.

Banks are open Monday to Friday 08.30–14.15 (some open Saturday 09.00–13.00). Most banks offer cash machine facilities for UK bank and credit cards including Eurocheque cards. Exchange bureaux are indicated by a Cambio symbol.

The higher exchange rate is only a good deal if the commission charged is not excessive.

DRESS CODES

The islanders are basically Catholic, and have been hurtled into modern living over the last 60 years, so it is respectful to them not to go into the bigger towns such as Arrecife and the old capital of Teguise or Puerto del Rosario wearing skimpy shorts and tops, or shirtless. This dress code is absolutely fine for the holiday resorts, however.

ELECTRICITY

The islands have the same voltage as the UK, but with two-pin plugs, so you will need to bring an adaptor. These are readily available in the UK at electrical shops or major chemists. If you are considering buying electrical appliances to take home, always check that they will work in the UK before you buy them.

GETTING AROUND

Car hire and driving The police are very kind, understanding and helpful, but they are very firm, so do uphold the law. As in the UK, drinking and driving is severely dealt with. Seat belts are compulsory, except in towns. Children under 10 must travel in the back of the car. Never park where you should not – yellow lines mean 'do not park here' – since they are very quick to tow you away. They have special vehicles called '*gruas*', which take the car to a designated place, normally difficult to find, and of course you have to pay to get it back. Never cross a solid line when on a slip road joining a main road – make sure you wait until you get to the

SPEED LIMITS
- Autovia (primary road) 100 km/h (62.5 mph)
- Carretera (A road) 80 km/h (50 mph)
- Built-up areas 40 km/h (25 mph)

dotted line part before filtering in. Remember to give way to traffic coming from your left when you are on a roundabout, and to go round it anti-clockwise. If your car uses unleaded petrol, you need '*gasolina sin plomo*'.

Most road maps are fairly accurate, but they have not caught up with the new road numbering system, whose numbers bear no relationship to the old. The original GC road numbers have been abolished and FZ road numbers are used instead on Fuerteventura, and LZ numbers on Lanzarote. 'Local' is a small country lane and exits are marked as prefix 'Km' with the relevant number.

Rules of the road Remember to drive on the right. Motorists must carry their driving licences, passports and car-hire documents at all times. Failure to do so will result in an automatic on-the-spot fine if you are stopped in one of the frequent road checks.

Roads In general, the road surfaces are good. Road markings are clear, but some of the traffic systems can be confusing when first encountered. Be aware that traffic priorities in these complex traffic systems do not always conform to your expectations: you might find a stop sign part way around a roundabout or even on a main highway.

Petrol This is inexpensive on the islands and petrol stations are frequent along main routes. Always fill up with petrol before heading off into the hills or the interior.

Parking Parking meters are usual in built-up or popular areas. Here the parking spaces are marked out in blue. Pay at the meter and display the ticket on the windscreen. Parking in side streets is generally allowed except where the kerbstones are painted yellow (or green and white in bus-stop areas). Illegal parking results in the car being towed away.

Useful words for drivers
- *aparcamiento* parking
- *estacionamiento prohibido* no parking
- *ceda al paso* give way to the right and left
- *circunvalación* ring road

Public transport Current bus timetables are available from tourist offices. A regular and reliable bus service operates on both islands. Like the spokes of a wheel, buses mostly operate directly into and out of the capital. This means a change of bus is often necessary to reach a particular destination. It pays to be on the early side since buses sometimes run marginally ahead of schedule. Not all services operate on Sunday. The Canarian word for bus, *guagua*, is pronounced 'wah-wah'. The main resorts are connected to the capital, Arrecife, with a frequent bus service, mostly half hourly.

Taxis Official taxis are easily recognized by the sign on the roof. Next to the sign is a light that shows green when the taxi is free. Generally, short journeys within town are not expensive, especially with four people sharing. The taxis are colour coded according to the district in which they operate. For longer journeys outside town, you should agree a price beforehand.

Ferries Trasmediterranea runs ferries once a week from Cadiz to Gran Canaria, Lanzarote and Tenerife. Trasmediterranea's UK agent is **Southern Ferries**. ✆ 30 Churton St, London SW1V 2LP ☎ 0870 499 1305 🖷 0870 499 1304 ✉ info@southernferries.co.uk 🌐 www.southernferries.co.uk. ❶ Early bookings are necessary for school holidays and at Carnival time (February). Tickets include all meals during the voyage.

Ferries and hydrofoils A complex network of inter-island ferries and hydrofoils links the seven main islands of the Canaries, and schedules change very regularly, so you need to check times locally. Most of the inter-island services are operated by **Trasmediterranea** 🌐 www.trasmediterranea.es or the **Fred Olsen Line**. Timetable details and on-line booking on: 🌐 www.fredolsen.es. The local airline, **Binter Canarias**, provides regular flights between the islands. Booking centre: ☎ 902 39 13 92 🌐 www.bintercanarias.es

HEALTH MATTERS

Chemists Easily recognized by the big green cross above the door with the word '*Farmacia*', chemists are very good on the islands, supplying everything you might need including antibiotics, which you can buy over the counter. The staff are always very helpful and knowledgeable – if you want something that they do not have in stock, they will normally get it for you very quickly.

Health hazards The sun is very strong at all times of the year so take great care with sunbathing, even when there is a cool breeze. Use high-factor creams initially and limit your sunbathing hours. Cover up at midday and in the early afternoon when the sun is at its highest. Remember, a slow tan is deeper and lasts longer. Do not let sunburn ruin your holiday.

Water Tap water is produced by desalination. It is not unsafe but does not taste good and is rich in minerals, which can cause upset stomachs. It is recommended that you drink bottled water.

Clinics All resorts have clinics where English is spoken, so if you have minor ailments or injuries it is often better and faster to go to one of these, rather than to the hospital emergency department. All have fully qualified doctors and nursing staff. However, they may not be able to accept the Form E111 or equivalent and treatment will have to be paid for.

THE LANGUAGE

The Canarians respond warmly to visitors who attempt to speak a little of their language. Here are a few words and phrases to get you going.

ENGLISH
General vocabulary

yes	*sí* (see)
no	*no* (no)
please	*por favor* (por faBOR)
thank you (very much)	*(muchas) gracias*

SPANISH (pronunciation)

ENGLISH	**SPANISH** (pronunciation)
You're welcome	*de nada* (deNAda)
hello	*hola* (Ola)
goodbye	*adiós* (adeeYOS)
good morning/day	*buenos días* (BWEnos DEEyas)
good afternoon/evening	*buenas tardes* (BWEnas TARdes)
good evening (after dark)/night	*buenas noches* (BWEnas NOches)
excuse me (to get attention or to get past)	*¡disculpe!* (desKOOLpay)
excuse me (to apologise or to ask pardon)	*¡perdón!* (perDON)
Sorry	*lo siento* (lo seeYENtoe)
Help!	*¡socorro!* (SOHcohroe)
today	*hoy* (oy)
tomorrow	*mañana* (manYAna)
yesterday	*ayer* (ayYER)

Useful words & phrases

open	*abierto* (abeeYERtoe)
closed	*cerrado* (therRAdoe)
push	*empujar* (empooYAR)
pull	*tirar* (teeRAR)
How much is it?	*¿Cuánto es?* (KWANtoe es)
expensive	*caro/a* (KARo/a)
bureau de change	*la oficina de cambio* (la ofeeTHEEna de KAMbeeyo)
post office	*correos* (koRAYos)
duty (all-night) chemist	*la farmacia de guardia* (la farMAHtheeya de garDEEya)
bank card	*la tarjeta de banco* (la tarHEHta de BANko)
credit card	*la tarjeta de crédito* (la tarHEHta de CREdeetoe)

ENGLISH	**SPANISH** (pronunciation)
traveller's cheques	*los cheques de viaje* (los CHEkes de beeAhay)
table	*la mesa* (la MEHsa)
menu	*el menú/la carta* (el menOO/la KARta)
waiter	*el/la camarero/a* (el/la kahmahRERo/a)
water	*agua* (Agwa)
fizzy/still water	*agua con/sin gas* (Agwa con/sin gas)
I don't understand	*no entiendo* (No enteeYENdoe)
The bill, please	*La cuenta, por favor* (la KWENta, por faBOR)
Do you speak English?	*¿Habla usted inglés?* (Ablah OOsted eenGLES)
My name is...	*Me llamo ...* (meh YAmoh ...)
Where are the toilets?	*¿Dónde están los servicios?* (DONdeh esTAN los serBEEtheeos)
Where is there a telephone?	*¿Dónde está un teléfono?* (DONdeh esTAH oon teLEfono)
Can you call me a taxi?	*¿Puede llamar a un taxi?* (PWEday yaMAR ah oon TAKsee)
Can you help me?	*¿Puede ayudarme?* (PWEday ayooDARmeh)
The police please	*La policia por favor* (la poleethee-a por fabor)
The fire brigade please	*Los bomberos por favor* (los bombearos por fabor)
An ambulance please	*Una ambulancia por favor* (oona amboolanthya por fabor)
There's been an accident	*Ha habido un accidente* (a abeedo oon aktheedente)
I am at...	*estoy en...* (estoy en...)
My telephone number is...	*Mi numero de teléfono es...* (mee noomero de telefono es...)

OPENING HOURS

General shopping hours are 09.00–13.00 and 17.00–20.00. Sunday is a
general closing day. Shopping hours are not rigidly followed, especially in
tourist areas. Supermarkets and bread shops are often open earlier,
usually at 08.30, and there are always some which stay open all day.
Many shops relying on the tourist trade stay open until late evening,
closing at around 22.00.

PERSONAL COMFORT & SECURITY

Complaints In a hotel, if all else fails and you cannot get a complaint
sorted out to your satisfaction, ask for the complaints book (*el libro de
reclamaciones*) Hotels are required by law to have one – you write down
your complaint and it is forwarded to the Spanish Ministry of Tourism.

Crime prevention Take as much care of your personal property as you
would at home. Watch out for pickpockets, especially in crowded market
places. Crime with violence is unusual, but do not take risks. Leave
nothing of value in a parked car, not even locked in the boot. Bag
snatchers are around, too, so carry your valuables in a bag securely
anchored to your body.

Lost property Report any loss or theft to your holiday representative. If
an insurance claim is to be made, you must report thefts within 24 hours
to the Municipal Police or Guardia Civil, from whom an official report
must be obtained.

Police If you have a problem – say with lost or stolen property – talk to
your holiday representative or hotel desk; they can help you make an
official statement to the police. There are basically 2 types of police force

TELEPHONING ABROAD

The dialling code for international access is 00.
Wait until a second dialling tone is heard, then dial the country
code (UK = 44), followed by the area code (without the initial zero)
and the subscriber number.

> **EMERGENCY NUMBERS**
> For an ambulance or help in an emergency call: ☎ 112

on the island: La Policia Municipal, who come under the local authority at the Town Hall (Ayuntamiento), are responsible for the law and order in the local authority area and also traffic control. They wear dark blue uniforms. La Guardia Civil (Civil Guard), who are responsible for law and order in the rural areas, and traffic control on main roads and cities. If you are committing an offence while driving, they are the ones that will stop and fine you. They wear green uniforms.

POST OFFICES

Many shops selling postcards will have stamps too. Remember that the post boxes on the islands are yellow. In the villages the opening hours of post offices are short, sometimes only between 11.00 and 14.00 hours.

TELEPHONES

Clear multilingual instructions are displayed in direct-dial telephone booths. Phonecards can be purchased from local shops and will save you having to carry pockets full of change to the public call box.

 The cheapest time to call home is after 20.00 hours on Saturday and all day Sunday.

TIME DIFFERENCES

There is no time difference between the Canaries and the UK. The clocks go forward in April and back in October simultaneously.

WEIGHTS & MEASUREMENTS

The metric system is used, as in the UK but you will not get a pint. A *caña* (pronounced kanya) is as near as you get to half a pint, and a *jarra* (pronounced harra) is as near as you get to a pint.

ACKNOWLEDGEMENTS

We would like to thank all the photographers, picture libraries and organisations for the loan of the photographs reproduced in this book, to whom copyright in the photograph belongs:
Barry Malone (Pages 49, 55, 91);
Doug Houghton/Alamy (Pages 25, 30, 69);
ImageState/Alamy (Page 16);
Isifa Image Service s.r.o/Alamy (Pages 10, 73);
Profimedia.CZ s.r.o/Alamy (Page 83);
John Henshall/Alamy (Page 89);
JupiterImages Corporation (Page 111);
Thomas Cook Tour Operations Ltd (pages 1, 5, 20, 37, 42, 53, 57, 59, 65, 67, 71).

We would also like to thank the following for their contribution to this series:
John Woodcock (map and symbols artwork);
Becky Alexander, Patricia Baker, Sophie Bevan, Judith Chamberlain-Webber, Nicky Gyopari, Stephanie Horner, Krystyna Mayer, Robin Pridy (editorial support);
Christine Engert, Suzie Johanson, Richard Lloyd, Richard Peters, Alistair Plumb, Jane Prior, Barbara Theisen, Ginny Zeal, Barbara Zuñiga (Design support)

Send your thoughts to
books@thomascook.com

- Found a beach bar, peaceful stretch of sand or must-see sight that we don't feature?

- Like to tip us off about any information that needs a little updating?

- Want to tell us what you love about this handy, little guidebook and more importantly how we can make it even handier?

Then here's your chance to tell all! Send us ideas, discoveries and recommendations today and then look out for your valuable input in the next edition of this title. And, as an extra 'thank you' from Thomas Cook Publishing, you'll be automatically entered into our exciting monthly prize draw.

Email to the above address or write to:
HotSpots Project Editor, Thomas Cook Publishing, PO Box 227, Unit 15/16, Coningsby Road, Peterborough PE3 8SB, UK.